G000269431

B⚏XTREE

It's the page that once got bummed in the bogs at Betty's Tea Rooms.

It's the page that rings your doorbell every time you sit down for a shit.

It's the page that has found a lump in its testicles, but would rather die than go to a lady doctor.

It's the letters page that's been undressed by kings, and seen some things that a letters page ain't supposed to see.

It's the page that once wanked into its granny's handbag in a moment of madness.

It's the page that spent the night coughing, and found a big grey pube in its throat this morning.

It's the page that spent double physics surreptitiously scoffing Coolmints - then shat itself on the way home from school and threw its pants in a bush.

It's the page that's got socks for Christmas and is trying to smile convincingly at its mum.

It's the page that once coughed a docker's omelette into its hand on the Bakerloo Line....
...and wiped it on a lady's coat.

First published 2003 by Boxtree
an imprint of Pan Macmillan Publishers Ltd
Pan Macmillan, 20 New Wharf Road, London N1 9RR
Basingstoke and Oxford
Associated companies throughout the world
www.panmacmillan.com

ISBN 0 7522 2503 0

9 8 7 6 5 4 3 2 1

A CIP catalogue record for this book is available from
the British Library.

Printed and bound by Proost

I am interested in buying a caravan. However, I cannot find the caravan that goes with my car. If anyone has a caravan with the license plate J471 PSD could I please buy it from them?

Paul McBeath, Southport

A different kettle of piss

If Mr Jameson or Mrs Houseman (my old head of year teachers) are reading this, I pissed in your staff room kettle.

Wayne Martin, Alfreton

If Ryan Giggs grew a 'Hitler' type tash he'd look like that bloke on the piano out of seventies group Sparks.

Jill W, Manchester

I'd love to buff up Samantha Janus's bullseye, winnits, clinkers and the whole dangleberry shebang.

Paul Harvey, Salisbury

I decided to save all my money for a rainy day. The next day it rained, and having saved less than £3, I spent it all on a packet of fags and a newspaper.

A. Brigden,
Liverpool

A trip down mammary lane

Whatever happened to seventies tits? Those plump, rounded, globby ones that stuck out sideways? Confessions films were full of them. Nowadays all you see is bouncing beach balls or tuppenny baps.

R. V. Window, Dunstable

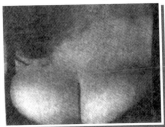

My son has very good contacts in showbusiness, and may be able to get girls, aged 18 to 30, highly paid work as actresses and models. Any young girl interested should send a photo of herself, posing topless, to my son at the following address: OM2 David Wooley, D23438U (3P Mess), HMS Southampton, BFPO 389. Thanks.

Mr T. Wooley, Beeston

Ugly Truth

They say that honesty is the best policy. Well the other day I told a motor cyclist in the pub that his girlfriend was boot ugly, which was the truth. In reward for my honesty I got a broken nose, lost eight teeth, and have suffered blackouts ever since.

P. Tart, Towcester

The person who coined the phrase 'as different as chalk and cheese' obviously hadn't tasted Kwik Save's cheddar.

John Sampson, Southampton

The Sex Pistols called for anarchy in the U.K. Well, if it's anarchy Johnny Rotten is after, why doesn't he go and live in Albania instead of dining on rocket and quail's arse salads with his poncy pals in Soho's Groucho Club.

T. Horseoftheyearshow, Wembley

Perhaps you could help settle an argument. My brother says that Hitler's hair was tapered at the back. But I insist he had a straight cut above the collar. Who is right?

Paul Noodle, Kettering

* Your brother wins the bet, Paul. As you can see from this photo, Hitler had a greased back graduated crop, tapered towards the neck. The extra body on top enabled a strong right parting and produced that famous swept fringe. It also appears to be hiding the beginnings of a bald patch which, had he not committed suicide in 1945, may have led to major 'Herr' problems during his planned period of world domination.

If EastEnders is so true to life, how come none of the loveable

Cockney characters are Man Utd supporters?

P. Sullivan, Birkenhead

Wasp a load of rubbish

What you don't know can't hurt you, or so we're told. Well, last week I didn't know that a wasp had crawled into my slipper, and it hurt me a great deal. Once again, the so-called experts get it wrong.

M.J. Bristow, Belfast

McTell it like it is

I wish the singer/songwriters of the seventies would get their facts right. In his sentimental ballad 'Streets of London', Ralph McTell sings "In his eyes you see no pride, hand held loosely by his side, yesterday's paper, telling yesterday's news".

Surely if they were yesterday's papers, they would be telling news from the day before yesterday.

Andrew Coughlin, Balham

I waited twenty minutes to use a toilet on a train from Minneapolis to Seattle last Christmas. When the occupant finally emerged I was surprised to see it was none other than publicity seeking entrepreneur Richard Branson. He didn't apologise for taking so long and left the cubicle stinking of millionaire shit.

A Coventry fan, Minnesota

Why do women keep telling me to go fuck myself? If I could fuck myself, I wouldn't be putting my hands up their skirts in the first place.

Heath Barrett, Tasmania

If the Fonz is so cool, why does he hang around with fuckwits like Cunningham, Potsy and Ralph Malph?

Robert Scott, Spalding

If Giles Brandreth were to have a sex change (which, as he is a Tory MP is not entirely out of the question) and the late Roy Castle were to rise from the grave and have unprotected sex with him, then I believe the resulting child would look a lot like the seventies American singer Ray Stevens. What do other readers think?

P. Sausages, Richmond

Whoever coined the phrase 'cleanliness is next to godliness' was talking out of his arse. I looked them up in the dictionary last night. Godly and godsend are next to godliness. Cleanliness was 343 pages away.

Jeff Hobbs, London

Don't trust the fogies

If shopkeepers only allow two kids into their shop at once in order to prevent shoplifting, the same rule should apply to OAPs. Never mind young and inexperienced shop lifters, these old people are seasoned and accomplished criminals.

I would implore shop owners not to trust old folk. They may appear harmless, but they have a lifetime of thieving experience under their belts.

David Southwell, Fleetwood

Honest John

People say that I am as honest as the day is long. Does this mean that in winter, as the days become shorter, I become proportionately less honest, and might therefore be tempted to start shoplifting, for example?

John (aka Ed) Sylvester, Rickmansworth

Anyone down on their luck and feeling depressed should take a trip to their local specialist comic shop. The sight of the assorted pond life gathered there, aged 12 to 40, discussing the upcoming Spiderman convention and cracking jokes in Klingon will put your own sad and sorry life in much brighter perspective. It works better than Prozac for me.

nm64cb, e-mail

Piss off the clowns

Unfortunately Europe's only circus school is just a unicycle ride from our local. As a result crusty, white, middle-class twats constantly turn up at the bar to demonstrate their fire juggling ability (or lack of it) and their 'clown skills'.

I've got nothing against kids with dreadlocks and public schools accents running away from their rich mummies and daddies to join the circus school. But can they please keep the fuck out of The Bricklayers Arms in Charlotte Road, London EC4? Thank you.

Loz and Jenna, London

I become incensed when I see opticians wearing glasses. These people should be sacked at once. What right have they to criticise other people's eyesight when they cannot see properly themselves?

Arthur Ritick-Joints, Stairlift-on-sea

They say football is a game of two halves. Not for me it isn't. I regularly down eight or nine pints whilst watching a live game on Sky TV in my local.

Adrian Bond, London

The magnificent spectacle of fox hunting need not be lost if the government decides to outlaw hunting. The dogs could quite easily be trained to hunt a pillow case full of sausages instead. When they eventually track down their quarry, they could rip it open and eat the sausages. The huntsmen could join in, cooking some of the sausages on a small, portable barbecue. And instead of blood, children hunting for the first time could have their faces smeared with mustard.

U. Bulgaria, Wimbledon

They say that an area of Brazilian rain forest the size of Wales is destroyed every year. What people forget however, is that Wales is only a small country, so small in fact that it only has a handful of professional football clubs, all of whom play in the English league. Brazil, on the other hand, are the current world champions. So what's the problem?

D. Tox, Chester

Monkey business

Don't invite chimps to your birthday parties. They drink tea straight out of the spout, and if you give them a bun they eat the cherry off the top and squash the rest. I know because I saw it happen in Leeds years ago. Or I had a dream about it. I can't remember.

Mark Mango Bingo, Pontefract

I see that this here 'orange marching season' is on again in Paisley country, and with it comes the usual problems. Why not give these patriotic marchers something useful to do? If the government built a giant treadmill they could march and march and march to their heart's content without burning anyone's house down. And their marching

could generate electricity which would be good for the environment too.

Paul Gardner, London

Free frock ops for OAPs

Men live to an average age of 70, whilst women carry on till they're 78. On my 70th birthday I fully intend to have a sex change operation in order to claim my extra 8 years. And I jolly well expect the NHS to pay for it.

H. Plasterboard, Huntington

It's a breeding liberty

Whilst visiting my local supermarket I was disgusted to find the best parking spaces nearest the door are now reserved for so-called 'Parent and Child Parking'. If these people are fit enough to procreate and produce offspring in the first place, they should jolly well be able to walk across a car park into the supermarket.

The best spaces should be reserved for the people with the most expensive cars. It is us who are likely to spend most money in the supermarket, and to have the most shopping to carry back to our cars.

B. Norris, Surrey

National No Car Day (June 17th) was a great success. There was absolutely nothing on the road and I was able to drive to my office in half the usual time. Let's hope this becomes a regular annual event.

B. Dog, Doodahband

With reference to the supermarket pricing label on the left. It is nice that Asda not only give cooking instructions with pre-packed food, but also brief descriptions of their staff too.

Little G., Brighton

Why do Japanese TV manufacturers deem it necessary to have a display on television sets that show us how loud the volume is? Surely people are capable of listening to the volume and deciding how loud it is for themselves.

Fintan Coyle, e-mail

Further to B. Norris's letter. If supermarkets continue to set aside the best spaces for 'parent and child' parking, surely this will only encourage young, impressionable teenagers to get pregnant on purpose so as to take advantage of these spaces. It's no wonder our younger generation are in moral disarray, when supermarkets use 'alcopops' to entice youngsters into stores and provide premium parking spaces for teenage mothers.

G. Sweeny, Wolverhampton

Advertisers claim that chewing gum is good for your teeth because it makes you produce more saliva, the natural protection for your teeth. Then how come Opal Fruits, which are made to make your mouth water, make your teeth rotten?

Tim Williams, Newport

11

My husband and I were very concerned when our son arrived home last night in a police car. Then I remembered, he is a policeman, and his partner always drops him off home after work.

Mrs B. Avern, Fulchester

Been around the world and I-I-I... can't find my luggage

It's a pity British Airways don't include baggage on their mileage based 'Frequent Flyer' programme. I checked my bags in recently for a short BA flight. By the time BA's bungling baggage handlers had finished with it, it would have earned enough points to win a place on the next space shuttle flight.

Convenour V.O.B.A.
(Victims of British Airways),
Australia

The water companies are always complaining about low water levels in their reservoirs. Well, I drive past my local reservoir every day, and each morning I fill a bucket of water from my tap and empty it into the reservoir on my way to work.

If all your readers did the same, these reservoirs would be full in no time.

Gordon Hall, Biscuits

If moths like the light so much why don't they simply come out during the day, instead of flapping about outside windows and crashing into car headlights all night long? Besides which, during the day, bats would not eat them.

Carl Hough, e-mail

He's still standing

Marc Bolan, a great friend of Elton John's, died tragically young in a car crash. Freddy Mercury, a great friend of Elton John's, was sadly taken from us by AIDS. Gianni Versace, a great friend of Elton John's, was cruelly cut down in the prime of life. And the Princess of Wales, so recently seen comforting Elton John at Versace's funeral, has ▶

What's the naughtiest thing you've ever done?

YOU CONFESS

Steve Jenkins, 22, dispatch rider

"When I was 16, I borrowed my dad's car without permission. I crashed it, and said it had been stolen."

Richard Turd-Burglar, 12, ad-sales manager
"When I was a teenager in Australia, I used to steal women's underwear from washing lines and wear it in bed."

Peter Sutcliffe, 53, lorry driver

"Between the dates of February 1977 and November 1980, in the counties of West and South Yorkshire, I attacked and killed 13 women"

Andy Turnbull, 32, coffee machine engineer
"Once while stopping at my granny's, I used her false teeth to wipe my arse with, then put them back in her mouth."

Headline News

- With reference to sub-editors slipping rude headlines into their articles, I think the cheeky staff at OK Magazine have done well here. Either that, or they have some real inside information.

  R. Donnett, Wimbledon

BARBRA STREISAND
HAS THE PAINTERS IN

Wendall Wall, the man Barbra Streisa accused of stalking her, is suing the d Last January ll was d by

SAFEWAY GOODIES - Page

School site: Parents opposed

MOBILE MAST DEBATE

- I spotted the above clipping too, only my letter arrived two days after R. Donnett's. Bugger.

  Daniel Fox, Cardiff

- What about this one (see right) from the Holyhead and Anglesey Mail. Sod the sub-headings, they've gone for the front page splash.

  Max, Beaumaris

been stolen from us. I'll tell you what. If I were George Michael I'd be shitting myself.

Andrew Cooke, Birmingham

Why, oh why does Jerry mouse's cousin keep sending his kids to stay with Jerry despite the fact that he is almost constantly being chased by Tom the cat? Invariably their holiday consists of nothing more than a non-stop series of cat and mouse chases from which they are lucky to escape unscathed.

G. Duffy, e-mail

If smoking is so bad for you, how come it cures salmon? Perhaps Tony Blair and his so-called 'New Labour' cronies could give us a straight answer to that.

Stalker, Bournemouth

No crust on his hairy pie

Professional 'oldie' Richard Ingrams makes a living complaining about young people and harping on about the good old days. But his preference for all things old stops short of the bedroom, where he has opted for a ripe young bird in favour of his wrinkly missus.

Lyn Hope, Spout

This is the order we would shag the Spice Girls in.
1. Posh Spice
2. Ginger Spice
3. Baby Spice
4. Scary Spice
5. Sporty Spice
Do any of your readers disagree?

Stu & Chas, Sheffield

Send your preferred order of shagging Spice Girls to: My Spice Shag Order of Preference, Viz comic, PO Box 1PT, Newcastle upon Tyne, NE99 1PT. We'll ask Jimmy Hill what order he would shag them in, and the first reader who matches his selection will get to take a penalty in the World Cup Final in France next year.

I stopped reading *Viz* two years ago, and since then I have started to suffer from agonising piles. I started reading it again last issue, and already my piles are much better.

**Abdul M.,
c/o The Acorn, Penzance**

I had to laugh when I heard a young boy talking to his mother in the zoo the other day. I'm a hyena.

A hyena, The zoo

Telescope for improvement

If Patrick Moore is such a good astrologer, how come he didn't see that tornado that ripped the roof off his observatory coming in the stars?

Mrs Victoria Terrace, Chigley

Had Jeanette Krankie been on board the Titanic she would have been the safest passenger on the ship. When they manned the lifeboats and the cry went out for "women and children first" she would have qualified under both categories.

Edward Semi, Norwich

It's snow joke

I went bobsleighing this Christmas. I killed Bob Holness, Bob Monkhouse and Bob Carolgees.

Do any other readers have jokes that work better when said out loud as opposed to written down?

Alex Walsh-Atkins, Birmingham

Sir Bob Geldof, who wrote the line 'There won't be snow in Africa this Christmas' has obviously never been up Mount Kilimanjaro.

M. Boardman, Stockport

Opponents of fox hunting foolishly suggest that drag hunting would be an adequate replacement for our sport. Well I for one would take no pleasure from hunting foxes dressed in women's clothing.

E.B. Poole Northumberland

I thought the local council had gone too far with their traffic calming measures when I drove over a 'sleeping policeman' on the drive outside my house. Then I realised it was my husband. He is a police officer and had nodded off in his deck chair after doing some gardening. Luckily, the doctors saw the funny side, although they tell me my husband may never walk again.

Mrs B. Idiot, Hove

Women secretaries have no sense of loyalty to their employers. They're happy to cash their pay cheques, drink your coffee and use your phone, but the minute you try giving them a quick Christmas bonus behind the filing cabinet they go straight to the police.

P. Hammond-Organ,
HMP Parkhurst, IOW

Doctor in the blouse

Women are a bunch of hypocrites. One minute they're carrying kidney donor cards around with them, quite happy to donate all their organs to medical research. But the minute a doctor or dentist tries to feel them up a bit while they're under the gas they go running to the police.

Dr P. Hammond-Organ
(struck off), Fulchester

If any of your readers are ever on a live television show featuring Uri Geller, and he asks you to draw a picture so that he can use his psychic powers to draw an exact copy, draw a picture of a big, hairy, veiny cock and watch the spooky bastard squirm.

James Lennox,
Glasgow

Spud-U-look like

With regard to interesting shaped vegetables. I've got a potato that looks like Alice Beer off Watchdog. Do I win £5?

Phil Crouch, Bourne
P.S. Come to think of it, I've got a whole sack of potatoes that look like Alice Beer off Watchdog. And a lemon.

I know this is supposed to be the year of the Tiger, but I'm still writing Dragon on all my cheques.

Mark Fung-Po, Stockport

I had to laugh at something my son said the other day. Mind you, he's Chubby Brown.

Mrs Ida Brown,
Middlesbrough

Wives no longer feel any sense of duty to their husbands. When they take their marriage vows

17

they promise to honour and obey you. But the moment you ask them to do a simple favour, like bring you a cake with a gun in it, they hand your letter to the prison authorities.

P. Hammond-Organ
High security 'E' wing
HMP Durham

Is anyone else as pissed off as I am about the famous acting McGann brothers? There must be about fifty of them, and every one is a fanny rat. No wonder blokes like me can't get a girlfriend.

Mike Pearson, Leicester

Why do they bother with soft porn? People that hate porn don't like it, and the people that love porn don't like it. So what's the point?

Sasha Shaw, e-mail

Several weeks ago I sent Denise Van Outen some of my pubic hair and a photocopy of my penis, yet she still hasn't had the decency to reply. Isn't it about time some of these so-called 'celebrities' looked down from their ivory towers and realised that it is borderline psychotics like myself who made them what they are today?

John Sowerby,
Sedbergh

Rude vegetables are getting a lot ruder nowadays, I can tell you. I enclose a photo I took in my arden recently showing a pair of root vegetables engaged in apparent 'golden shower' shenanigans.

John Tait, Thropton

18

Mice to Big 'C' you, to Big 'C' you, mice

So scientists claim to have found a cure for cancer in mice. Big deal. That's great news if you happen to be a mouse.

Why don't these idiots try finding a cancer cure for people? After all, it's us who pay their wages through our taxes. Not mice.

Mrs G. Day, Cullercoats

You often see signs outside churches telling us that 'Jesus Lives'. But these religious folk are always carping on about how he died on the cross for all our sins. Dying isn't much of a sacrifice if you're planning on coming back again five minutes later.

Come on, God botherers. make up your minds. Is he dead or is he alive?

Mr S. Turd, Corbridge

I had to laugh the other day. I was sniffing nitrous oxide.

T. Paddock, Sedbergh

The answer is blowing in the wind

A few days ago in bed a bottom burp of my husband's brought forth the unmistakable words "POL-POT." the following morning I awoke to hear the news that the infamous leader of the Khmer Rouge had died. Last night my husband farted in the bath. It's not looking good for Edward Woodward.

Mrs Tinkle, Sebsy

Who says we're not getting a good deal from our train services since privatisation? Admittedly the fares have increased out of all ▶

19

That's Shelves!!!

I've got a shelf that's two metres long. Can any of your readers beat that?

King Shelf, Newcastle

I put up a shelf the other day, and the wife said it didn't look straight. Imagine her surprise when I checked it with a spirit level and it was perfectly horizontal. It was an optical illusion! How we both laughed.

Arthur Twoshelves, Daventry

The things kids say! "Look, grandad, that mantlepiece has lost its fireplace," my 3-year-old grandson said the other day. He was pointing at a shelf! Do I win £5?

Ernie McShelf, Kinross

I won a really nice shelf in a raffle, but everything I put on it falls off. That's because I'm a lighthouse keeper or I live in a windmill, and the only way I could fasten it on the wall was to fit it vertically!

Eamonn O'Shelf, Edison Rock Lighthouse, Amsterdam

I haven't got any shelves in my house. That's because I work in a supermarket stacking shelves, and the last thing I want to look at when I get home is more shelves!

Rosemary Shelfson, St Asaph

That's nothing. I work in IKEA, stacking self-assembly shelves... onto shelves! If I came home and there was more shelves in my house, I'd probably flip, murder my wife and kids, and then turn the gun on myself!

Billy Bookcase, Gateshead

The things kids say! "Grandad, why has that shelf got four legs?" my 3-year-old grandson asked me in the kitchen the other day. He was pointing at the table! *Now* do I win £5?

Ernie McShelf,
Kinross

I've been collecting shelves for forty years. "I've bought you something to help you store your collection," my wife said the other day. "I hope it's not another shelf," I replied. It was a box!

Sheldon Elf
Matlock Bath

All you shelf fans are saddos and wrinklies. They haven't even got doors. Get with it and get cupboarded up!

Kurt Cupboard
Cirencester

Miriam

SHELF HELP WITH MIRIAM STOPPARD

Dear Miriam...

This Christmas, my boyfriend bought me a pair of bookends to put on my shelf. He'd overlooked one fact; I don't have any books. However, I have got twelve videos which occasionally topple over, especially when I'm dusting. Do you think it would be okay to use these bookends as "video-ends" instead?

Sarah, Luton

Miriam writes...

My ex-husband playwright Tom Stoppard's old woodwork teacher always used to tell him to never use a tool for any purpose for which it wasn't intended. However, in this case I think you can safely ignore that advice. Your bookends will make marvellous "video-ends" to stop your tapes toppling over!

21

‣ proportion and the journeys are often hours longer that they were ten years go, but the fine for pulling the emergency brake is £50, exactly the same as it was in 1962. That's what I call value for money.

Foz, Tottenham

What's the big Ikea?

Following Ikea's ad campaign 'Don't be so British', I think suppliers of crap British flat-pack furniture should use the slogan "Don't be so Swedish". The ads could feature clips of Swedes hanging themselves, supplying arms to the Nazis and wanking over farmyard animal pornography.

J. Terry, Hebburn

Having worked for many years in the tropical diseases department of a large teaching hospital, I have seen first hand the terrible effects of water-borne diseases that wreak havoc on the digestive system. Having said that, I had to laugh when I heard that Esther Rantzen had contracted amoebic dysentry.

Dr C.N. Cornflakes, Battersea

I'm as liberal as the next man, and I've got nothing against them personally, but I really don't think it's a good idea for the Prime Minister to fill his cabinet full of gays. The last thing Mr Blair wants as he sits there with his finger on the nuclear button is Nick Brown and Chris Smith wandering up behind him and stroking his hair.

T. Kavanagh, Wapping

Fraud of the dance

Why does everyone make such a fuss about Michael Flatley and his Riverdancing? There's nothing clever about dancing if you've only got to think about moving your feet. Proper dancers like Lionel Blair wave their arms all over the shop. I think Mr Flatley should charge half as much as he does for his tickets.

Mrs H.N. Loops, Rhyll

In the bible, why do they always use a capital 'H' on He or Him or His when refering to God, even if it's in the middle of a sentence? Does he get annoyed if you spell it with a little 'h' like I just have, and if so, what's he going to do about it?

R. Brek, Kidderminster

Desperate measures

So the EU is clamping down on Suicidal Syds by ruling that no more that 16 paracetamols can be bought at one time. The next thing you know, they'll be ruling that rope can only be bought in 1 metre lengths.

G. Lewis, Abadare

In reply to Mrs Loops' letter about Michael Flatley. What she fails to realise is that although Michael Flatley only moves his legs, they actually go three times faster than Lionel Blair's. This means that his tickets are actually two thirds the price that they ought to be.

Mr Frosties, Luton

What a lot of nonsense is talked about being run over by buses. My grandfather was run over by his first bus when he was 12 - and he was run over 80 times a day until he was 104, when he was killed by a cigarette.

G. Nuggets, Warrington

I've just been struck by an enormous bolt of lightning. I am covered in boils and my house is full of frogs. I strongly recommend that when referring to God, always use the upper case 'H' on all personal pronouns.

R. Brek, Kidderminster

I read in an article recently that one third of road accidents are caused by people who have been drinking too much, and one quarter are caused by people driving too quickly. It doesn't take a genius to work out that too thirds are therefore caused by people who have not had enough to drink, and three quarters by people who drive too slowly. This means that people who drive quickly whilst over the limit are twelve times safer than those who are sober and obey the speed limit.

David Clayton, My Bog

I had to laugh the other day. It was in the script.

Noel Edmonds, Crinkly Bottom

Roll up, roll up

I've just had a massive shit, then noticed that there isn't any toilet paper. If either of my parents, who are avid *Viz* readers, happen to be reading this, could you please throw a toilet roll up onto the landing.

J. Tudor, Sheffield

Why does Prince Naseem get a gong just because he's good at punching people? I'm brilliant at it but the most I've ever got is 200 hours community service.

A Woodward, Sheffield

I think it's a disgrace that the hard shoulder on motorways is reserved for broken down vehicles or accident victims. Why should irresponsible motorists who can't be bothered to look where they're going or service their car enjoy the privilege of their own lane? It's madness gone mad. I suggest that in future the hard shoulder should be reserved for cars with a full service history, and no dents.

Mark Glover, Coventry

If my vicar genuinely believes that it is better to give than to receive, why doesn't he put his hand in his pocket and stick £100 on the collection plate next Sunday? The congregation can do the receiving for a change.

G. Salmon, Sheffield

Nobody ever comes to Cyprus just once", so the tourism advert says. My dad did. He was ran over and killed by a bus in Limmasol on the first day of his holiday.

I. Porterfield, Sunderland

I reckon my dick looks like Bobby Charlton. Does anyone else have a tonk which looks like a celebrity?

Tyrone Shoelaces, Bolton

What a load of rubbish this new 'foil wrapped bread' is. It's supposed to last for 7 days. I ate mine in two. Do I win £10?

Chris Pether, e-mail

24

See you, Jimmy

I spotted Jimmy Hill, not in *Viz* but on this saucy seaside postcard where, in response to an enquiry about cucumbers, Jim humorously alludes to the size of his penis and implies a sexual attraction to the female customer.

Miss S. Hall & the sandwich boy, Jesmond

Jimmy Hill seems to be manifesting himself everywhere. Not content with appearing in the *Viz* or brandishing phallus-shaped cucumbers on saucy postcards, he appears on the pages of popular Scottish cartoon 'Oor Wullie' dressed as a rabbit. Thankfully, Wullie hadn't dropped acid, he'd only eaten cheese the night before.

Alan Donnelly, Croydon

Pop the question

If it's true what they say, "Once you pop, you can't stop", why are Pringles tubes resealable?

A. Bean, Sudbury

25

Monumental error

Britain is littered with war memorials dedicated to "those that have laid down" and "those who have fallen" during two world wars. Has anybody considered building a monument to the poor sods who weren't bone idle or too clumsy to keep their footing and who actually got shot?

W. Donachie, Dundee

Why do our media and politicians often refer to the evil Iraqi dictator Saddam Hussein simply as 'Saddam'? You could hardly imagine Iraqi TV broadcasting a message to the people of Baghdad saying "Last night we were bombed again by George and Tony".

Neil F. Mayell, London SE12

Den of iniquity

Not so Dirty Den now," says Leslie Grantham on that new soap ad. It must be good if it's washed the blood off his hands.

Big Bean, Edinburgh

Honourable member

In response to your request for readers with dicks which resemble celebrities. I have the good fortune to be circumcised, and by the addition of a miniature pair of spectacles, fashioned from a pipe cleaner, I can transform my member into a dead ringer for right-wing labour MP and unfounded cannibal rumour victim Gerald Kaufman.

Graham Brook, Wilmslow

They say that good manners cost nothing. Bollocks. I sent my daughter to a posh finishing school in Switzerland, and it cost me twenty bastard grand.

J. Morgan, Wigan

I wish the irresponsible makers of ITV's "Don't Try This At Home" would stress the title of the show a little more. Only the other day I arrived home to find my wife ▶

Don't ask me I'm dead!

with Dr. Magnus Pyke

Send your queries to Magnus Pike, 'Don't Ask Me I'm Dead', Viz, PO Box IPT, Newcastle upon Tyne, NE99 1PT.

❑ Is it true that water goes down a plughole in a clockwise spiral North of the Equator, and the opposite way round in the South? If so, why? And what happens if your bath sits directly on the Equator?

Mr H. Alexander
Pontefrct, West Yorkshire

❑ *Don't ask me Mr Alexander. I'm dead.*

❑ Why is it that my fingertips wrinkle like prunes if I am in the bath for more than ten minutes?

Mrs J. Pinder
Oxford

❑ *There's a very simple answer to that Mrs Pinder, but I'm afraid I'm still dead.*

Bum Notes
-Britain's LIVELIEST tramp correspondence column

Each issue, **Bum Notes** asks for *YOUR* opinions on a different aspect of tramps. Here's what you had to say about this week's Tramp Topic... **Begging**

...in my opinion, simply buying the Big Issue only goes part of the way in solving the problem of homeless people begging. What I do is roll up my copy and strike them smartly across the nose, saying 'NO' in a firm, clear voice. Like my dog, they'll soon learn not to beg again.

Jane Rowlands, market researcher

...begging for spare change in the street must be very humiliating. For this reason, before I hand over my 10p, I make the tramp do a little dance for me and my friends. That way, he has provided a service and has **earned** the money, thereby gaining some self respect.

John Wilson, librarian

...if a tramp asks you for some money for a cup of tea, chances are they'll go and spend it on cigarettes and beer. Mind you, I've got an off-licence, so I say give it to them.

F. Welsh, shopkeeper

...begging is antisocial behaviour and will not stop until the public take a firm stand against beggars. When asked for change, I let these people know in no uncertain terms that they will get nothing from me by quickening my pace, looking at my shoes and mumbling 'sorry, no'.

Aiden Clifford, graphic designer

...most of these beggars are just con men. I was once about to hand over 10p to one unfortunate looking fellow when suddenly a mobile phone rang in his pocket. I couldn't believe it! It was the garage telling him that his car was ready. A Rolls Royce, if you please. And a solid gold one at that. With mink seats!

Charles Lewethwaite, retired brigadier

and children attempting to drive a Mini Moke across a rope bridge suspended between two hot air balloons at 30,000 feet. With a snake in their pants. On fire. Etc. In our living room.

John Tait, Thropton

Bearing in mind the outcome of recent murder investigations, might it not be an idea for the police launching new ones to simply hold a press conference and arrest the first person who starts bubbling?

C.L., Fife

Surely there was no need to move the News at Ten to make way for all-action Hollywood blockbuster movies. Trevor MacDonald could simply have read the news whilst on fire, being blasted through a large pane of sugar glass by a huge fireball explosion, flailing his arms and legs pointlessly. In a vest.

M. Radcliffe, Ipswich

In Holland Park the other day I passed the headquarters of the Esperanto Society - who campaign for the world-wide adoption of their own universal language. However, I couldn't help wondering what language they would use to shout out of the window if the building caught fire. I somehow think that "Assisti! Assisti! Propra domo est je fajr," would not be the first phrase that sprang to their big fat hypocritical lips.

S. Dennis, Clifton

If, as Freddie Mercury claimed, fat bottomed girls make the rocking world go round, isn't it about time that the city of Derby received some recognition for its contribution to astrophysics?

Neil Sedgwick, Nottingham

Public service announcement

Iwonder if I could use the pages of your magazine to relay a message to Matt Coomber who has been on holiday in Australia for the last six months.

Matt - if you are reading this, phone your mum. She wants to know if you still want all the jazz mags she's just found in your bedroom.

Ian Warren, London

Owners of smoke alarms - where's your sense of adventure?

Heron Bailey, e-mail

Rod Hull. It finished 1-1 by the way.

Moose, Southampton

Esther Rantzen said in the Sunday Telegraph that an unpleasant child is a contradiction in terms, and that she'd never met a child she didn't like. Obviously she's never come home and found some 13 year-old Rat Boy shitting on her living room carpet with her video under his arm.

Mrs A. Hedley, Byker

Smiles better

They say that laughter is the best medicine. My grandad has got Parkinson's disease and we've been laughing at him for months and he hasn't got any better. So much for that theory.

D. Smoog, Paris

Why do farmers always put their gates right next to the muddiest parts of the field?

Neil Bye, e-mail

Mum's the work

Why don't all these so called single mothers employ another single mother as an au-pair? Then they could all get proper jobs.

M. Withkids, Surbiton

Jonathan Ross should be ashamed of himself. All the money he's got and his daughter gets bitten off a snake. I earn just over £100 per week and my daughter has never been attacked by a reptile. My son once got stang off a wasp, but that was when I was on income support.

Mrs G. Yarwood, Halesowen

Jerry Hall says that to keep your husband keen, you must be a 'maid in the parlour, a cook in the kitchen and a whore in the bedroom.' I recently decided to follow her advice. I kept the house very clean, I prepared delicious meals every night, and I allowed dozens of fat businessmen to have sex with me for money in the marital bed. Surprisingly, my husband left me. Did I follow her advice correctly?

Pauline Riley, e-mail

With regard to Pauline Riley's letter (opposite), Jerry Hall is talking out of her Texan arse. The perfect woman is obviously going to be a whore in the parlour, a whore in the kitchen and a whore in the bedroom. And then she can think about getting my tea on.

R.T., Kilburn

In this century Britain has only made war with countries whose capital cities begin with the letter 'B' - Germany (Berlin), Argentina (Buenos Aires), Iraq (Baghdad) and Serbia (Belgrade). China change the name of Peking to Beijing and we bomb their embassy. One hopes in the new century we will show a little more imagination when making war with other nations.

Martin Harwood, Bradford

If a woman says no she means no, but if she tells me she's over 16 then it's my call. Where's the justice?

S. Partridge, e-mail

The death of Rod Hull has proved to be a bit of a disappointment for me. I originally misheard the news report and thought they said ROY HUDD. Imagine how sad I was to hear that the old cunt was still alive.

G. McKendrick, Glasgow

These so-called speed humps are a joke. If anything they slow you down.

Tim Wakefield, Surrey

I wouldn't trust him as far as I could throw him" my mother used to say about my father. But then we are a family of travelling acrobats, so I assume it meant she could trust him quite a lot.

Chris Mapperly, e-mail

If the waitress in the Bardon Mill Little Chef is reading this - please will you clear away our empty plates and take our pudding order?

S.L. Marston, Table 6

Why is it that people never seem to fight on top of trains these days?

Justin D., Cobram, Australia

Big 'C' down under

It's nice to see a star like Robbie Williams fronting the British 'Testicular Cancer Awareness Campaign'. Here in Australia, we have to make do with a cartoon of Mark Hughes checking his pills in a shower.

Mick Noble, Brisbane

Hi. How it going? Lars Grenninger is my call. The *Viz* is my funny read ever since years three ago. Laugh! Yes my sides broken good with the giggle. I search friend to write. My likes are cycling, read books and dinosaurs, ten inch cock. Bye.

L. Grenninger, Spitsbergen

Something ought to be done about Britain's so called Fat Cats. My husband works a seventy hour week as a security guard and comes home with less than £150. Meanwhile, the woman next door has got a cat that weighs three stones and never does anything, just eats butter out of the fridge and shits in our flower bed. Where's the fairness in that?

Mrs B. Kramer, Hull

On our wedding aniversary this year, my husband promised to treat me like a princess. And he was as good as his word. He took me out for a meal, got completely pissed and on the way home crashed the car into a concrete pillar at 120mph, killing me instantly.

Mrs B., Essex

My old Dutch oven

Now I've been going out with my girlfriend for some time, it seems to be okay when I break wind in bed. It's when I follow through that the petty arguments begin. I will honestly never understand women.

Chris Mapply, Carshalton

So Michael Portillo has come out of his filthy closet and now intends to stand for the seat left vacant by the sad death of Alan Clark MP. I am a life-long Tory, but I will not be voting for this bouffanted nancy boy. I don't want to see the Mother of Parliaments defiled by the sight of a man wearing false breasts and a dress mincing up to the despatch box, dragging a chair and limply examining surfaces for dust.

T. Kavanagh, Canary Wharf

False romance

So this film Romance claims to be the first in Britain to contain scenes of actual, rather than simulated sex. What a load of rubbish. I saw Confessions from a Holiday Camp in 1978, which contained a scene where scouse actor Tony Booth shagged a woman in a toolshed so much that the shed actually fell to pieces. If that's not real sex, I don't know what is.

P. Mackay, Fife

Iwas watching golf on telly the other day and I realised that even the top players take two or three swipes at the ball before being able to hit it. I'm not one to complain, but I'm not sure they are completely worth the millions they receive.

Dave, e-mail

Rip-off Van Rental

Ineeded to move a wardrobe last week and telephoned a van hire company to ask the cost. I was staggered when I was told it would be £8000. How I laughed when I realised I had misdialled, and by complete coincidence had rung Van Morrison's agent. Do I win £10?

S. Hayes, Wigan

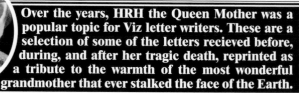

Over the years, HRH the Queen Mother was a popular topic for Viz letter writers. These are a selection of some of the letters recieved before, during, and after her tragic death, reprinted as a tribute to the warmth of the most wonderful grandmother that ever stalked the face of the Earth.

I'VE got 58 pence to my name and I live in a cardboard box behind a bus shelter in Peterborough. With her huge overdraft, the Queen mum is £4 million worse off than me, yet she lives in 5 castles. I'm not a communist or anything, but I wonder if someone could offer me an explanation.

Charlie, Peterborough

I'D like to wake up next to the Queen Mum the day after her 100th birthday, give her a big kiss and order the butler to bring champagne to celebrate a right-royal night of centegenarian bedroom games.

Neal Pearce, Horsham

ENOUGH about the Queen Mum's 100th birthday, I want to know who, or what, has been servicing her love tunnel over the last fifty years. If she has been screwing around, then this is in clear breach of Christian teachings on love and marriage and needs to be exposed. If she has been indulging in regular self-abuse, then what kind of example does this set the rest of us?

Mr. Fox, Shoreham

I'D like to slap the Queen Mum's bum and watch her crinkly arse-cheeks explode with pleasure.

Neal Pearce, Horsham

WITH the Queen Mum just celebrating her 101st birthday, wouldn't it have been glorious for the country if someone had painted a number 1 on her left arse cheek and a number 1 on her right. She could then have bent over, spreading her glorious, yet mature arse cheeks to display 101, broadcast live to the nation. That would have been a birthday to remember.

Sir Fingerbobs, Turkey

IF THE Queen Mum (God bless her) really was the nation's favourite grandmother, why aren't we seeing any of her cash? She left ninety-odd million, and as far as I'm aware, us adopted grandchildren are getting fuck all in her will.

John Paul O'Kane, e-mail

I WAS saddened to learn of the death of the Queen Mum, whose remarkable life was one dedicated to the service of her country and her family. Her galvanising devotion to duty put the other freeloading, layabout royals to shame. Imagine my disappointment then, when I learned that she died peacefully in her sleep at 3.15 on a Saturday afternoon. What the hell was she doing in bed on a Saturday afternoon? The lazy bitch.

U. Helmet, e-mail

WE HAVE heard many tributes to the Queen Mother, saying how above all, she had time for people. Well she never had any time for me. I was her dentist.

Graeme Kenna, Wallasey

WHILST there will inevitably be those who attempt to get a 'cheap laugh' out of the death of the Queen Mother, we should remember her tremendous contribution to the war effort. As the BBC pointed out, she "bravely remained in London beside her husband" during the war. This contrasts sharply with the actions of my own grandfather who on the declaration of war immediately left his wife and children and pissed off, first to France, then North Africa, Italy, France (again) and finally Germany. The shame will always be with me.

George Nisbet, e-mail

I WAS shocked to hear that after her death, the Queen Mother's coffin was in turd at Windsor Castle. Surely it would have been more respectful to bury her in soil.

R. Savage, Berwick

THE FUNERAL of Her Majesty the Queen Mother was indeed a sad and sombre occasion. The BBC, by using David Dimbleby as the commentator, added to the sombreness and added to the nation's grief. If they had asked Murray Walker to do the commentary, his fast talking would have made the funeral exciting, and his humourous gaffes would have kept us laughing through our tears.

Martin, Yorkshire

WE WERE all greatly saddened by the death of the Queen Mother, but let's look on the bright side. With the clocks going forward the night after she popped her clogs, she has already 'lost' an hour of being dead.

Guy, Nottingham

SO Prince Charles thinks the Queen Mum was a 'truly magical grandmother' does he? Well, I'd have thought my granny was pretty magical too, if she lived in a big fairytale castle and travelled everywhere in a gold coach with a platoon of her very own living toy soldiers to guard her.

Madra, e-mail

LIKE THE Queen Mum, my grandfather was a frequent visitor to the East End during the dark days of the blitz, but he was never hailed as a hero by the people of London. That's because he flew Heinkel bombers for the Luftwaffe.

Werner Hoffmann, Munich

Monkey business

I recently paid £10 to drive around The Marquis of Bath's Safari Park at Longleat. What a farce. If any of your readers see the marquis, perhaps they might like to clamber all over his car, waving their arses in his face, pull the rubber trim off his windscreen and shit on the back of his window, see how he likes it.

J. Kidd, Frampton on Severn

M y daughter got married last year, and I called a company to enquire about the cost of hiring a marquee for the day. I was staggered to be quoted a price of £8000. How I laughed when I realised I had dialled the wrong number and was actually talking to the agent of 'Mark. E.' Smith out of The Fall. I'm sorry to go on, but I really do need £10, honest.

S. Hayes, Wigan

I 'm a bunch of squaddies stationed in Bratislava and I...erm, we are dying to see a picture of the lovely Anita Harris with her kit off. Failing this, is there any chance you could cleverly graft her head onto any naked bint using that computer stuff. I... we have searched the internet for the above, but to no avail. Can you help?

Tom Spaghetti,
18/30 Lancers

* *Here you go, Tom. All done with scissors and glue, and 'Anita' job you couldn't wish for.*

Gas bag

W hen I was nine, my best mate Jon and I threw a Calor gas container into a bonfire for a bit of a laugh. My next door neighbour phoned the Fire Brigade who arrived just in time to pull the canister out before it exploded. She's always been an interfering old bitch, but as for the Fire Brigade - haven't they got anything better to do?

L. Andrews, Surrey

I would just like to say a big thankyou to all those wonderful young people who stand on motorway slip-roads (in any weather, mind you) holding up boards telling us motorists where they lead to.

B. Bollockbrain, Braintree

May I just say that not everyone who watches the Miss World contest on television is a slobbering sexist. Some of us think that in these cynical times it is refreshing to hear beautiful girls so concerned about the environment, elderly people and world poverty. The fact that they are wearing skimpy costumes barely concealing their vibrant, rounded breasts and tantalising us with the briefest glimpses of shaven bikini lines covering their mounds of pleasure is totally irrelevant.

Paul Dixon, Northumberland

Blue blood

So your Royal Family are worth the millions they cost because of all the tourist dollars they bring into the country? If they were really committed to boosting tourism, they would strip naked and perform depraved sex shows on the balcony of Buckingham Palace. I wouldn't travel round the block to see your Queen changing the guard, but I'd fly halfway round the world to see Lady Melons Windsor licking out Sophie Rhys-Jones whilst getting ridden up the ass by Zara Philips with a 10-inch strap-on. Hot diggety!

Chuck Schwartzheimer, San Francisco

When will greengrocers stop referring to 'New Potatoes'? They've been out for years now, so isn't it about time they just called them potatoes?

T. Doyle, Dagenham

British readers may be interested to know that the other day I saw 'Harold' off Neighbours walking around Melbourne. And I can tell you he looks a very different person. Off screen he is painfully thin, a foot taller and sports a moustache, but he still wears his unmistakeable coke-bottle glasses. At least I think it was Harold off Neighbours.

Justin Deegan, Cobram, Australia

These so-called disposable cameras are such a farce. Now I have absolutely no record of a perfectly lovely holiday.

S. Partridge, e-mail

Hopping mad

I am a Flea Circus owner and recently decided to groom my performers for a big show. I chose 'Johnsons Dog Flea Shampoo', but far from cleaning my fleas' hair, it actually killed them. Let this serve as a warning to other flea keepers.

D. Miller, Kiphill

Don't try this at home

Davina McCall says that dangling off a helicopter over the Grand Canyon on a 700 foot bungee rope was the most terrifying and dangerous thing she has ever done. She must be forgetting that she went out with Stan Collymore.

M. Duckworth, Poole

Desert island dish

A recent survey named Carol Vorderman as the woman most men would want to be stranded on a desert island with. I think a more sensible choice of 'Girl Friday' would be Sharron Davies, as she could suck you off and then swim for help.

Spud, Luton

Jugged Aries

I think astrology is a pile of shit. My girlfriend is an Aries and she's got tits like two thruppenny bits on an ironing board. Meanwhile, her younger sister, who is also an Aries, has got the biggest pair of paps I've ever seen. I'd like roly-poly astrologer Russell Grant to explain that if he can.

Andrew Nesbit, e-mail

Father of the Millennium award must surely go to David Beckham. Unlike many fathers, he is prepared to endure excruciating pain to have his son's name tattooed in fancy Old English capitals across the top of his arse. I doubt many of his critics would show a similar love for their children.

J. Vance, Cardiff

It's good to stalk

Psychologists tell us that it is practically unheard of for stalkers to attack the objects of their obsession. This must be some comfort to the 50% of The Beatles who haven't been shot or stabbed.

J. Van der Lande, Den Haag

As a mincing homosexual, I am utterly sickened by the fact that the perfectly good word 'gay' is being hijacked as a socially acceptable term for 'happy' by retired, purple-faced army Majors who read the Daily Telegraph. I for one will not allow these tweed-clad buffers with their handlebar moustaches to stop me using the word in its proper context, meaning 'on the other bus'.

J. Wilson, London

I smoke 80 a day, but I am unable to take any comfort from from the statistics that say I am just as likely to be ran over by a bus as I am do die of lung cancer. That's because I live on Sark.

R. Le Feuvre, Sark

I don't know what Roy Castle is complaining about. I got cancer of the ears from listening to trumpet records in a fag factory.

T. Evans, Pitlochrie

So Sting is able to shag his wife for five hours without going off. I know how he feels. My wife is no oil painting either.

J. Leonard, Hull

Thought you might like to know what goes on in the Cotswolds.

Pete Coulton, Heaton

In the frame

My favourite 'You've Been Framed' clip is the one when that bloke is waving cheerily to all those people from his car, completely unaware that he's about to be shot in the head. The look on his wife's face!

Chuck Wanker Jnr., Des Moines

Sick note

I visited my local GP last week complaining of a sore throat and stiff neck. Imagine my surprise on being told I had absentmindedly swallowed a flute.

Danny Keough, Exeter

Parcel of crap

I heard recently that on average, Her Majesty the Queen receives two turds in the post each week. What I want to know is, who's sending the other one?

F. Jacks, Hartlepool

To call Dr. Harold Shipman 'Britain's Worst Serial Killer' is utter nonsense. With more confirmed kills to his name than any other UK-based murderer, surely Dr. Shipman is 'Britain's Best Serial Killer'. Someone like Colin Stagg who not only was arrested in connection with only one killing, but then turned out not to have done it in the first place, would qualify at the country's 'Worst Mass Murderer'.

Danny King, Balham

With the recent hospital slip ups, I can understand how a doctor amputates the wrong arm or leg, or removes the wrong organ. As arms and legs come in pairs, and are therefore easy to confuse, perhaps the nurses could put a glove or a sock on the limb to be removed. As for internal organs, well we will just have to take our chances.

P.M. Maiello, Llanelli

What a complete hypocrite Paul McCartney is. He won't eat sausages, but he's quite prepared to have ivory on his piano keyboard, oh Lord. Does he really expect us to believe that if they made pianos out of sausages, he'd suddenly start eating elephants again? Frankly, I think not.

Brigadier Sir J. Lewthwait, Cumberland

Smile, Please!

● I was reading in-flight magazine *Skyline* the other day when I came across this picture of Judith Chalmers trying her best to squeeze out a grin at an awards ceremony. *'Wish I Wasn't Here'*, she appears to be thinking.

Neil Henderson, Shetland

● In response to your request for incincere smiles, I spotted this one whilst flicking through Food Trade Review. It's a smile to start with, but looked at for a second or two, it turns into a rather threatening snarl. Scary.

Sarah Newman, Prestwich

Have Your Say

We went on the streets to ask your views on whether, in the wake of the Queen Mum's death, should Prince Charles marry Camilla Parker-Bowles?

...I THINK Charles and Camilla should have married before the Queen Mother died. She would have loved to see her favourite grandson happy, and we could have seen some great camcorder footage of the old girl flashing he bloomers whilst dancing and falling over at the reception.

...I WOULD love it if they got married, just so I could see the Queen pull that fucking face she pulls, the one as if someone has just farted.

...CHARLES WOULD be the first to admit that he made mistakes in his marriage to Lady Di, mistakes that he would not make again. If he married Camilla, he certainly couldn't sneak off and poke someone uglier than his wife.

...I HOPE they don't get married. If they had a son, with his ears and her teeth, the next in line to the throne could be a fucking rabbit.

...I THINK they should get married. Let's not forget that Camilla's cousin is 'Who Wants To Be A Millionaire' winner Judith Keppel, and she'd buy them a fantastic present like a diamond encrusted toaster or a solid gold fondue set.

...PRINCE CHARLES is 54 and he still lives at home with his mum. He should get married straight away before people start to think that he's a lifter like his brother.

The other day I looked at my calendar and, noticing it was July, put on my swimming trunks and flip-flops and set up the paddling pool for the kids. How foolish I felt when my wife reminded me that I was an Eskimo and live in year-round sub-zero temperatures.

Ron Stubbs, North Pole

We are constantly having to see 'clammy bottoms' on nappy adverts these days, so how about seeing some of those fine young models on the Tampax adverts actually sticking their products up their minges. I for one would much prefer to see some second-rate actress's biff close up than have to see a baby's piss-soaked arse while I'm eating my cornflakes first thing in the morning.

Rhydian Lewis, Porthcawl

Bearing in mind the large amount of pornography available on the internet and the forthcoming free internet access, now would be a prudent time to invest in shares in tissue manufacturers and companies that make sore-knob cream.

John Hunt, Edinburgh

Once a loony leftie, always a loony leftie I say. If the people of London are foolish enough to elect Ken 'Red' Livingstone as their Lord Mayor, they will have no one to blame but themselves when the lesbians and the IRA are winning all the sandcastle and snowmen competions in the park.

M. Compton, Bristol

Amen corner

The padre of Manchester United football club says he prayed to the Lord as his team were 1-0 down in the final seconds of last year's European Championship. With 2 goals in the last minute, his prayer certainly seems to have worked. If he can spare a few minutes after asking God to fix matches for his team of 11 millionaires, perhaps he could put in a word on behalf of the millions of sick, starving and dying all over the world. Just if he's got time.

Wilfred M. Thompson, Penrith

So a spoonful of sugar helps the medicine goes down, does it? Well I'm an insulin dependant diabetic, and after following this advice, I am now two months into a life threatening hyperglycaemic coma. Thank you very much, Mary fucking Poppins.

Elron Hubbard, Bradford

I tried to write my name on a sock recently using a sharp pencil, but the pencil went straight through and cut my foot. Small bespoke name tags are much better for this purpose and are available from my shop.

A. Lee (Gents Outfitter) Ropergate, Pontefract

My mate prefers a Snickers Bar to a Mars Bar. But strangely, he prefers Mars ice-cream to Snickers ice-cream. The hypocrisy of the situation annoys me no end.

Bickbucks McCoy, e-mail

The government safety campaign proclaims 'Speed Kills!' What nonsense. As an astronaut, I regularly travelled at 30,000 mph on space missions and came to no harm. The Titanic was doing less than 30 mph when it hit an iceberg killing over 1,500 people.

Neil Armstrong, Houston, West Yorkshire

Blankety blanker

What a small world. For example, there appears to be two Terry Wogans. The one in the TV Times, criticising the BBC for paying big name presenters inflated salaries at the expense of quality programming, and that other one who gets £550,000 a year to front shite like Auntie's Sporting Bloomers.

Richard Hauptmann, Chester

What a con these so-called radio controlled taxis are. I got in one the other day and there was a man inside driving it.

J. Beneaux, Leeds

It seems that you cannot open a newspaper today without seeing

44

stories and pictures of David Beckham and Posh Spice splashed all over the place. Do the editors ever stop to wonder if anyone is actually interested in the mundane comings and goings of these overpaid and underworked, self-important idiots who seem to be famous simply for being famous? The space could be put to much better use with more stories about the Royal family.

A. Richards, Burnley

Brits oot!

Saucy singers, such as Shania Twain and Britney Spears are all enjoying successful careers at the moment. But the sooner we stop buying their albums, the sooner they'll go broke and be forced to make porn films to pay their bills.

Antony Peterson,
New Zealand

Woof justice

It seems very unfair that people brand certain dogs as 'dangerous'. These dogs spend less that 1% of their lives mauling children and babies, and yet they are branded as dangerous. 99% of the time they are not savaging anyone. If your car worked 99% of the time you would not call it 'unreliable'. Maybe it's just that I've never been scared of dangerous animals. I was once bitten on the arse by a German Shepherd, but he apologised afterwards and even introduced me to his dog.

Stewart Ferris, Chichester

These days it seems politically incorrect to be in favour of capital punishment. I'm all in favour of the death penalty for murder, but only in cases where they are absolutely sure that the convicted person is guilty. In other cases where there is a bit of doubt, they could be given life imprisonment, and life should mean life.

T. Houston, Southport

With the increasing number of near-misses and mid-air collisions over our skies, it's high time that the airlines started fitting bumpers to their planes, especially now that some of them allow women 'pilots'.

Stewart Ferris, Chichester

Christmas seems to come earlier every year. My next door neighbours have already got a Christmas tree growing in their garden - in February! It's absolutely ridiculous.

J. Bishop, Oslo

I am fed up with people describing Formula 1 as "the most glamorous sport in the world." Having studied sport the world over, I have to say that a couple of topless Page 3 birds wrestling in a vat of custard is a lot more glamorous.

H. Jego, Kidderminster

I read T. Houston's letter with interest and came up with a better idea. Anyone found guilty of murder should be hanged and then the bodies could be frozen, like Walt Disney's. Later on when they are found not guilty, they could be thawed out and brought back to life using a fu-

ture technology which will probably be available by then.

R. Brown, Great Yarmouth

Meat the wife

My local butcher's shop is so clean, you could eat a raw sausage directly out of the butcher's trouser pocket. I know this because I spotted my wife doing it in the back of his shop the other day and she seems to have suffered no ill effects.

Hector Johnson, Bournemouth

Slow thinking

With the FIA constantly looking for ways to slow down modern Formula 1 cars, why haven't they tried wrapping hair and fluff around the rear wheel axles? It certainly works on my Scalextric.

J. Gash, e-mail

I've donated over a thousand pounds this year to the World Wildlife Fund. Imagine my anger when I saw them fighting over the money on satellite telly, rather than spending it on vanishing tigers in Sumatra.

Charlie Hamilton, e-mail

46

Check it out

I used my credit card to pay for £32 of groceries at Tesco's recently and the woman on the till asked me if I wanted any cashback. I requested £20 which she cheerfully gave me. So my shopping really only cost me £12. Who says the supermarkets are ripping us off?

A. Berry, Grimsby

Ladies' darts nights in pubs around the country could be improved by scrapping the usual game of 501, and just going straight for double one, which is where most games finish anyway. The time saved could then be spent drinking more heavily than usual and fighting in the car park.

Neil Hanson, e-mail

Why do old people insist on referring to World War I as 'The Great War'? Surely World War II with its higher death toll and use of atomic weapons was loads better.

G. Delaney, London

There's no pleasing my wife. She complains when I leave the toilet seat up, she complains when I leave it down and piss all over it.

Jon, Leeds

I went to sign on the other day and was told that I couldn't have any money due to the fact that I was in full time employment. If this government think I'm going to give up a perfectly good job just to get hold of their poxy dole, they must be stupid. Now wonder this country is in such a bloody state.

Alan Wade, Stockport

We shall fight them on the beaches, we shall fight them in the fields and on the landing grounds," said Churchill in 1939. Unusual use of the word 'we'. I was on Omaha Beach having my leg shot off and I can't remember seeing Winnie anywhere. Perhaps I missed the bit where he said "We shall fight them 50 feet underground in a reinforced concrete bunker."

S. Whiting, Carlisle

During the recent petrol crisis, I sat for over two hours in a queue at my local Esso station. I was furious, as I only wanted to buy a Mars bar and a paper.

Langy, Twickenham

I'm a driver, but the rising cost of fuel prices doesn't bother me as I always put £10 worth in my tank.

Lost his name, Sorry

These wind farms are ridiculous. As if this country doesn't have enough wind of its own without wasting electricity making more of it by running these big fans. It's a waste of the taxpayer's money.

Ben Cormack, Isle of Eigg

I was awoken the other morning by a rattle at my letterbox. It was my son, Simon Rattle, the conductor of the Birmingham Symphony Orchestra, who had forgotten his keys.

Mrs. Rattle, Birmingham

The other day, I rushed round to my neighbours' house to warn them of the kangaroo in their garden. Imagine how silly I felt when they explained it was just their greyhound having a shit.

Matthew Walker, Worcester

Praise the landlord

With alcohol-related crime rising and church attendance dropping, isn't it about time Tony Blair converted a few churches into pubs? I for one would be a lot less punchy if there were a few more pubs around that I wasn't barred from.

Guy, Nottingham

I couldn't agree more with J. Beneaux when he slags off radio controlled cabs (issue 102). And those 'Self-Drive' vans are no better. I hired one last week and settled down for a nice kip. When I woke up four hours later I was still outside the hire centre. Of course the AA were useless as ever, and when they couldn't find anything wrong I ended up having to steer all the way while they towed me to Skelmersdale.

L. Maas, Carnbee

I'm fed up with people moaning about the recent floods and complaining that their councils did little to help. My dad was caught in a flood and he didn't just sit on his fat arse waiting for the council to bring him some sandbags. He got his finger out and built a bloody great boat and filled it with animals. Not bad for a six-hundred year old.

Japheth, Mount Ararat

In a recent interview, Pamela Anderson expressed her shock at having her 'Honeymoon video' stolen, and admits she has never seen it herself. Well if she wants to get in touch, she can borrow my copy, just as soon as all my mates have finished watching it.

John Pala, Darlington

There's no pleasing some people. A couple of weeks ago the news was full of people moaning on about being flooded. These people would be the first to complain if they didn't have any water at all.

J. Lester, Derby

Given the current strains on the penal system, surely lighter, more jokey type sentences could be introduced for 'lovable rogue' type criminals.

Big Nige, Wakefield

A brief waste of time

Every time I check my answer machine messages, there's always one from Professor Steven Hawking, informing me of the time and day that he called. No offence to Mr Hawking, but I feel his messages are a waste of tape space. He should get back to solving the mysteries of the universe and leave me alone.

Ben Cormack, Castle Douglas

Mr. Muscle loves the jobs you hate', the advert says. Oh yes? Well I haven't noticed it volunteer to suck my husband's sweaty cock every Friday night when he comes up to bed after watching Eurotrash.

Mrs. E. Gaines, London

I was amazed to see the incredible prices of personalised car regis-

49

tration plates in an advert recently. However, Halfords kindly did me a set of "AN 1" for £15, saving me about £20,000.

Adrian Newth, Worcester

Can I just inform your more ignorant readers that not all lorry drivers are murderers. Some of them are just rapists.

Timbo, Hull

Iwas clearing out my shed last week when I found The Lord Jesus Christ, son of God stuck in a corner behind the lawnmower.

S. Paine, e-mail

Ham & eggo

Can any of your clever dick readers explain to me why the 'protective atmosphere' sliced ham is packed in smells like somebody has just farted in the packet. Or do you not care about what goes on in sliced ham packing factories?

M. Hunt, e-mail

Iam sick and tired of hearing wannabe TV and radio stars moaning on about how difficult it is to break into the world of showbiz. You never hear proper stars like Lisa Tarbuck and Zoe Ball complaining, do you?

By the way, who is Gail Porter's dad?

Jim, London

My grandad was the best drummer who ever lived, despite only having biscuit tins for a drum kit and two rolling pins for sticks. Although he had a poor sense of timing and rhythm, he compensated with a heavy handed playing style and practised enthusiastically for 18 hours a day. My Nan didn't appreciate his skills, however, and after 50 years of pounding, she stabbed him in the throat in 1985.

Darren Jarvis, e-mail

No wonder there is so much voter apathy. Politicians ask us to vote with our feet, then place the ballot box high on a table in the voting booth. With that prospect in mind, no wonder people choose to stay at home.

Ade Smith, Basingstoke

On the knocker

I wonder if I could use your letters page to warn women about a scam that is going on. If a man comes to your door and asks to look at your tits, claiming to be doing a survey, do not show him your tits. I fell for this the other day, and it was only later I discovered that there was no survey, he was only trying to see my tits.

B. Harrison, e-mail

I wish disabled people would stop moaning on about there being no access to public buildings. They get to sit in their wheelchairs whilst being carried up and down large flights of stairs - the rest of us have to walk.

W. Walker, Norwich

I recently watched Comic Relief's Red Nose Day on TV and was horrified by some of the humour. Frankly, I found the comedy shorts on Africa to be in rather poor taste. Call me old-fashioned but my idea of something funny is a man falling down a hole, or being hit in the face with a custard pie.

Ben Cormack, Isle of Eigg

I was reading Razzle this morning and I couldn't help thinking that if these were the readers' wives, no wonder they read jazzmags. Didn't stop me throwing some dripping over them, though.

Mike Barman, e-mail

Can anyone tell me the basis upon which the Queen's Birthday and New Year's Honours are awarded? Tory politician Norman Lamont is awarded a peerage and Eddie George, governor of the Bank of England is knighted. It seems farcical. Frank Bruno could floor both of them with one punch, and he only gets an OBE.

P. Geils, Oldham

Thyme for a wee

Whilst cleaning Jamie Oliver's windows the other day, I pissed in his window box with herbs in. Have any of your other readers done spiteful things to celebrities?

OTG, Herts

You'll never guess what happened to me. I travelled on holiday to Holland and forgot to take my coat - and it rained every day for a fortnight! Luckily I had taken a spare one along with me.

J. Rackham, Oxford

Why is it when nutters hear voices, they are always telling them to go out and kill women? Why don't they ever tell them to do something a little less extreme, like wash the car or give the missus a hand with the ironing?

M. Robson, Northumberland

Why is it every time I take a chimpanzee into my house, it puts fucking butter in my shoe or something? I've a good mind to stop letting chimps into my house.

Alan Mogarry, e-mail

They say that Jennifer Lopez is sexy because she's got a big arse. Well if that's the case, my girlfriend is at least twice as sexy as her.

Richard Harrison, Gwynedd

Court out

Whilst listening to Radio 5 Live a few weeks ago, I heard the reporter say that the Wimbledon Tennis Championships were just around the corner. Imagine my disappointment when I walked to the end of my street, only to find a dog being sick under an abandoned Ford Escort.

Stitch Mitchell, East Bradford

Peter Sutcliffe could be released from Broadmoor Mental Institution if he were made to wear a little bell round his neck. This has certainly worked on my cat which used to kill no end of birds, but has not killed one since I fixed it to his collar.

A. Carabino, Fulham

Scaramouche, Scaramouche, did he kill the Jill Dando?

On the face of it, it seems that Barry Bulsara has been convicted of Jill Dando's murder on the flimsiest of circumstantial evidence. After his conviction, however, certain facts came to light that paint a picture of a man quite capable of committing such an act. The sad fact is, that we may never know the truth of his guilt or innocence, because only one man knows for certain whether or not Bulsara is Jill's murderer, and that is Bulsara himself. Well, him and the bloke who actually did it, obviously.

Christina Ratcliffe, Hull

With reference to the letter from the man who pissed in Jamie Oliver's window box (previous page), that's nothing. Five years ago I worked as a baggage handler at Manchester airport. One day I saw Ulrika Jonsson checking her suitcase in for the Heathrow Shuttle, so I made my way down to the baggage hall and awaited the 'prize bag'. As colleagues kept watch, the bag was thrown to me inside the aircraft container and I put Ulrika's knickers on my head forthwith. As I opened her washbag and took the top off her Ladyshave, I was awestruck to see a solitary golden pube adorning the razor foil. At this point I was rushed by my excited colleagues just as I was about to put the beauty in my mouth for safe keeping.

I also once bent Gladiator Wolf's golf clubs through 45° and poured a tin of aircraft engine oil on Stan Boardman's suit. Blame that on the fucking Germans, you gap-toothed cunt.

A. Fairuz, e-mail

Recent reports show that far from costing the country money, Her Majesty the Queen actually brings in £10 million a year. Instead of trying to abolish the Monarchy, why doesn't the government turn all the unemployed into monarchs, thus creating a net income for the country of £10,000 billion pounds annually. That's a tax free windfall of £170,000 for every man, woman and child in the country.

D. Milligan, Jesmond

Film bluff

The other day whilst listening to Radio 5 Live, the presenter informed anyone who enjoyed action-packed movies, that the film Tomb Raider, starring Angelina Jolie would be right up their street. Imagine my disappointment when I found the same dog being sick under the same abandoned Ford Escort.

Stitch Mitchell, East Bradford

I saw the inside of a wheelchair-bound driver's car the other day and was astounded by the modifications that had been made to allow them to drive safely on the road. What if the same amount of time and trouble had been spent designing a vehicle specially made for a drunk driver? I'm sure the market for this sort of car would be huge. So come on, car manufacturers, get your thinking caps on and make our roads safer.

Edd Hillman, e-mail

Why are the police spending so much time and money collecting names for the national paedophile register? Surely they could just ask for a copy of the membership lists of all British caravanning clubs.

AMN, e-mail

For peat's sake

Please can someone help me? I can't seem to think of another purpose for multi-purpose compost, other than for growing plants in.

Leo Stitch, e-mail

Manufacturers of Dulux 'Once'. I think the word you are looking for is 'twice'.

K.C. Jones, Steaminanarollin

You treat your dad like he was a taxi driver!" my mum complained the other day. And I had ♦

Just ask Walt's head

Each week, you put __your__ questions to Walt Disney's head in a fridge

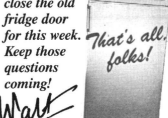

Dear Walt's head... Where is the coldest place on earth?

Rusty Junior III
Talahassee, Georgia

Well, I sometimes think it's the end of my nose! Brrrrr! But seriously, Rusty, it's probably Alaska or Iceland, or some place real chilly like that.

Dear Walt's head... Why do stars twinkle?

Mary Beth Kozwalski
Hell's Kitchen, NYC

That's a tough one, Mary Beth. I guess it's all the dirt and pollution and stuff in the skies that makes those little fellers twinkle so. Ahtchooooo!

Dear Walt's head... Why does a snail leave a silver trail?

Chuck Jerkoff Jnr.
Des Moines, Iowa

Well it helps them slide right along. See, those little critters, why, they carry their houses around on their backs, and that's a mighty tall order when you've only got one foot. Jesus H. Christ, it's cold in here.

Dear Walt's head... Does the light go off in a fridge when the door is closed?

Junior Ableman III, Jnr.IV
Flagstaff, Arizona

Well, little buddy, If I had a dollar for every time someone has asked my head that question...! Yes, it sure does.

Well, my head is starting to thaw out, so we'd best close the old fridge door for this week. Keep those questions coming!

That's all. folks!

Walt

55

Don't Ask Me.
I'm
Still Dead!
with
Dr. Magnus Pyke

□ Why is it that when I boil an egg it goes hard, yet when I boil a potato it goes soft?

Mr H. Woolf, Bristol

* *Don't ask me, Mr Woolf. I'm still dead.*

□ How come if I look at myself in a mirror I'm the wrong way round, but if I look at my husband on the telly he is the right way round?

Mrs P. Sissons, West London

* *I'm sorry, Mrs Sissons. I'm still dead.*

*Send your queries to Dr. Magnus Pyke at our usual address. Dr Pyke regrets that he is dead, and queries cannot therefore be answered

♦ to admit she was right. I'd just shot him in the back of the head.

Leslie Grantham,
Walford

Sorry states

The United States and Britain have finally apologised for their part in the slave trade in the 18th and 19th centuries, and so they should. But in the spirit of going forward, shouldn't certain African tribes apologise for cooking vicars in enormous metal cauldrons and stealing their top hats?

B. J. Holmes, Rhyll

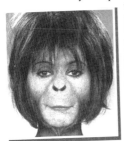

I was amazed to read how much money was spent on make up for the film Planet of the Apes. Surely they could have replaced Helena Bonham-Carter with that woman who plays Gail in Coronation Street and saved a fortune.

Andrew Dunn,
e-mail

A sign outside my bookmakers says 'Open every Sunday 11-5' Now I know for a fact that he is open on Sunday afternoons but he won't take my bet.

Dave Stuttard, Warrington

Webbed feat

According to National Geographic magazine, spiders' web silk is so strong that a strand the thickness of a pencil would be able to stop a Jumbo jet in flight. That is an amazing fact, but what is even more mind boggling is how strong a spider's nipsy must be to crimp the stuff off.

K. Dong, Prestatyn

There has been a proliferation this summer of car stickers informing us that 'Dogs Die in Hot Cars'. Thanks to this advice, I saved £45 in vet bills when I had to have my alsatian put down when it got distemper.

D. Haslam, e-mail

I had a dream last night that I had used the last piece of toilet roll. Today, after having a morning 'log out', that very same scenario occurred for real. It's reassuring to know, that in this time of misery and uncertainty, dreams do sometimes come true.

Becky Morris, Australia

I found this picture in an American phonebook a while ago. Take a look at it for a few seconds then turn it upside down and cover the glass and the lady's head.

Has anyone else found any hidden porn in phonebooks?

Kev Pryor, Leicester

J. FLOORING
01273 697...

I have been following the debate about lorry driver serial killers with interest. I run a large international lorry firm and therefore have a reputation to keep and standards to maintain. As well as insisting my drivers wear a tie, they are required to paint the names of any women they have killed on the front of their lorries. If I find a driver with 3 or more names on the cab, they get their P45 immediately. I will not employ serial killers.

Eddie, Cumbria

Who says doing Christmas shopping early avoids the crush? Last year, I did mine a full 12 months in advance, and the shops were just as busy as ever.

Gavin McKernan, Ballycastle

People should not say horrible things about the terrorist Osama Bin Laden. They are simply bringing themselves down to his level.

H. Francis, Cardiff

The Big Issue would sell a lot more copies if they made their vendors smarten up a bit. Most of them look like tramps.

Tim Woods, e-mail

Carlos driving

Rally driver Carlos Saintz ran through a crowd of 12 people at 100 mph and got a trophy. I ran through a bus queue and got 12 months, and I was only doing 65. It seems that there is one law for the foreigners and one for us.

J. Barnwell, London

Not content with dragging his granny round a supermarket in an advert, arsehole chef Jamie Oliver is now getting his sister, his mum and his dad in on the act. How many more of his family are going to jump on the gravy train? I dare say when him and Jules have a baby it'll be milked for all it's worth. And he'll probably write a book on cooking for toddlers. I don't know how he will have the nerve.

J. Raynor, London
P.S. And if he calls that book 'Tot Nosh', he's an even bigger twat than I thought.

On the subject of Jamie Oliver, I watched the fat-tongued mockney on telly preparing a dish using 'the old chicken' with a dash of 'the old lemon' and a hint of 'the old tarragon'. You'd think with his money he'd be able to use fresh ingredients, not ones past their sell-by date.

Bobby Harrison, London

I am not interested in the porn industry at all, and I wonder if Channel 5 are planning to show any documentaries not about the porn industry in the near future.

J. Sykes, Hull

So it's our car, our flat and our money, but I notice it's always her tits. There's feminism for you.

Neil, e-mail

If I understand it correctly, Osama Bin Laden's two main achievements so far have been to reduce airline prices, and to stop Americans leaving their country and clogging up ours. So what exactly were we bombing him for? We should give him a fucking knighthood.

Tim Woods, e-mail

Hair today, hair tomorrow

Whoever said Queen guitarist Brian May has not changed his hairstyle since the seventies is talking nonsesnse. If you compare the two photos (above), one taken in 1971 and the other in 1999, it is perfecrly obvious to anyone that today's style is slightly flatter on the top.

Windsor Holden, Chichester

I am sick and tired of your letters page branding all us truckers as serial killers. For your information, to be classed as a serial killer in the UK, one has to have murdered three or more people (Gekowski, 1998). Having only murdered two people (both of whom were female hitch hikers), I feel I am owed an apology.

Jared, Burton upon Trent

Why slaughter and incinerate livestock with foot and mouth disease when they can be redeployed to clear the world's mine fields?

Simon Hollingworth, Norwich

I am a burglar, and recently, whilst in the act of nicking a load of stuff from an old widow's house, I tripped on the edge of her rug, spraining my ankle quite badly. I was unable to burgle for three months, so I called that Accident Help Line. They fixed me up with a greedy, manipulative lawyer who got me £50,000, as her carpet should have been better secured to the floor. All that and her pension book too. What wonderful times we live in.

Ben Cormack, Isle of Eigg

I see Golden Wonder have a new promotion for their Pot Noodles - if you find a poodle in your Pot Noodle, then you win ten grand. When I opened one of the beef and mushroom flavoured snacks yesterday, I didn't find a poodle in the pot, but it looked and smelled like one had been in there for a shit.

Tim Robson, e-mail

I fancy having a bit of rabbit for my tea tonight. Could anyone tell me if it's cheaper from a butcher's or a pet shop?

J. Picklay, Worcester

Brought to book

J K Rowling makes much of the fact that she was a single mum on benefits whilst writing her first Harry Potter book. Well, if she was receiving benefits whilst writing, she was technically working, as she was doing it with a view to making money from her quaint meanderings. It follows, therefore, that she is one of the benefit cheats that the government are so keen to crack down on. If anyone would like to report her, the number to call is 0800 854440.

G. Brandolani, e-mail

I would just like to say good on Barrymore for bouncing back to our screens. Good riddance to the days when a troubled, alcoholic drug-addled, middle-aged homosexual would be banished from hosting a prime-time, family TV show merely for having a drugged, sexually injured corpse fished out of his swimming pool amid rumours of foul play.

Matthew Edwards & Mark Rowland, East Croydon

I thought all your readers might like the fact that the Prime Minister of India is called Hairy Vadge Pie, or something like that.

Ian MacKinnon, e-mail

They say one swallow doesn't make a summer. That's bollocks. I got this great nosh off a bird last April and I was still smiling in December.

Jon Wainwright, Chester

Miriam

ANSWERS YOUR PROBLEMS IN CHINESE

Dear Miriam... **I'm sixteen, and recently on holiday I had sex with this boy.** He told me you can't get pregnant the first time you do it, but now I've missed my period. Please don't tell me to go to the doctor, as he's a family friend and I'm terrified he'll tell my mum. Help me, Miriam. I don't know which way to turn.

MB, Kidderminster.

Miriam says... トナー容器も、こ ます。感光ドラムと廃棄トナー容器は していた箱に入れてご返却ください。 ジ色のトレイに差し込んでください。 器に付いている栓でふたをしてくださ リッジの郵送方法に従ってください。 ます。感光ドラムと廃棄トナー容器は

LETTER OF THE DAY

感光ドラムと廃棄トナ ます。感光ドラムと廃棄 していた箱に入れてご返 ジ色のトレイに差し込ん 器に付いている栓でふた リッジの郵送方法に従っ ます。感光ドラムと廃棄 していた箱に入れてご返

● ● ● ● ● ● ● ● ● ● ● ●

Dear Miriam... I'm 28, and married with two young children. I recently started work in a large office. The other day my boss asked me to stay behind after work to help him with some

62

filing. However, when we were alone he made a pass at me. I made it clear that I wasn't interested but he told me that if I didn't give in to his demands, I'd be looking for another job, so reluctantly I performed oral sex on him in the photocopying room. I was sure my husband was going to find out, as his best friend is my boss's siamese twin and he saw everything. However, he now says he won't tell my husband if I'll go with him to a stables and have anal intercourse with a horse. My boss says he'll sack me anyway if he discovers I've been going with a horse. My husband is a murderer and he's threatened to murder me if he finds out what's been going on, and also if I lose my job. I think the horse is HIV positive. Please help me Miriam, I am starting to lose sleep worrying about this.

JS, Reading

Miriam says... 感光ト

According to Newton's law, energy cannot be destroyed or created, only changed from one form to another. So why are all these boffins predicting we will one day run out of power? If you ask me, it's just another con trick by the gas board trying to stick their prices up.

Gavin McKernan, Ballycastle

If the Americans can't find Osama Bin Laden, they should stop looking, sit down with a cup of tea and try to think where they saw him last. This always works when I can't find my car keys or glasses.

M. Ross, London

You've got fe-mail

The other night, I dreamt I was boning Connie, the AOL girl. Imagine my delight when she took some speed and asked me to do bum games.

A. Skraga, e-mail

When I make comments about the size of Britney Spears's tits and women not making good pilots, my girlfriend accuses me of being sexist. Yet when I punch her in the face she starts ranting and raving about it being wrong to hit a lass. The hypocrisy of it all dumbfounds me.

M. Hobson, Whitley Bay

Ex-Arsenal fan Osama Bin Laden has taken football hooliganism to new extremes with his attack on New York. It makes me hanker for the good old days when they just threw coins and darts at each other.

H. Monroe, Wigan

Arsene Wenger said that Osama Bin Laden, an ex-Arsenal supporter, would not be welcome at Highbury again. Perhaps they should put a photograph of him on each turnstile, so that if he should attempt to get in he can be reported to the police.

J. Miles, London

A notice on the back of a tube of Colgate toothpaste says 'We do not make toothpaste for anyone else'. Imagine my anger when my friend's tube of Colgate had exactly the same notice.

Danny Handley, West Midlands

I am a lesbian trapped in a man's body. I am desperate to meet sympathetic women (preferably couples) who understand my plight, to see past the curse of penis affliction and initiate me into the joys of lesbian love. Please, please reach out and help a sister in distress.

Paul Murphy (aka Ethel),
e-mail

They say lightning never strikes in the same place twice. Nonsense. She caught me sniffing her leotards in her dressing room backstage at the Gladiators 1996 final, and she kicked me twice in the nuts.

S. Amias, Saint Albans

A recent report from the University of Chicago said that women are attracted to men that smell like their father. Well I'm not. My dad's been dead for three months and he must fucking ming.

Jane Harris, London

Anne Robinson was recently voted Britain's worst dressed woman. What about the pissed-up bag lady behind our local bottle bank, who shits her pants on a twice daily basis and recently set her coat on fire? She must have come second.

J. Carlisle, Exeter

Hobo-erotic

I think that the Big Issue would be better off producing jazz mags. This would mean that if your wife discovered any of your 'specialist literature' you could merely claim that you were helping the homeless.

Luke Robson-Smith,
e-mail

I understand that Dr. Harold Shipman received 15 life sentences for his wicked crimes. I think it is digusting! Why should he be allowed to live 15 times longer than anybody else?

Ian Iro, Ilkley

As Professor of Applied Biochemistry at Guys Hospital, I cannot agree with the findings of Prof. Alan Lucas at Great Ormond Street Hospital when he says that "breast is best". I have always been an arse man.

Prof. Stanley Jordan,
Guys Hospital

Genie with the light brown ale

Last Tuesday, while sat on a park bench drinking Special Brew from a bottle, a genie appeared and offered me 3 wishes. I wished to be sick, become incontinent and get arrested. Imagine my surprise the next morning on waking up in a police cell to find that all 3 wishes had come true.

T. Paddock, Millthrop

I was devastated the other day when my boss called me into his office and said he was going to fire me. I broke down in tears and begged him to reconsider. Imagine what a fool I felt when I suddenly remembered that I am the human cannon ball at the circus, and my boss was merely offering to help me practice. Do I win £5?

John Townsend, e-mail

They say that a dog is a man's best friend. Rubbish! My best friend is Ken Finch.

Lee Prescot, Widnes

It appears that Tesco are saving money on artwork. Viewed this way up, this logo is for strong onions. But turn it upside down and it's the logo for family sized hairy pie.

The Elves, Surrey

The other night I dreamt I was shagging the blonde one out of ABBA. It was the worst experience I've ever had to endure. Why the fuck I couldn't have dreamt that I was shagging his gorgeous wife Agnetha instead, I'll never know.

Angry Bob, Blackpool

Whoever says that mobile phones will one day completely replace the telephone kiosk is talking utter nonsense. Have they ever tried to piss into a Nokia 8210, or smear an unwanted kebab on the inside of an Ericsson T65?

A. Tern, Fulham

The legend of Bigfoot, a humanoid ape-like creature living in the Rocky Mountains of America was first told by the native Red Indians centuries ago. Due

to the vastness of the terrain, it is quite possible that such a creature could live undiscovered. Obviously, however, it could not live for centuries, so it follows that there would have to be a breeding population.

Based on my own field studies, I have calculated that the area where the bigfoot has been spotted could support around two hundred individuals. Just imagine if we captured all these magnificent beasts and trained them to perform Michael Flatley's Riverdance. What a show that would be!

T. Fletcher, University of Denver, I have a dream

Wankabout

Whilst driving in the middle of nowhere in the Australian outback recently, one of my tyres blew out. Considering myself pretty much fucked, my mood was brightened when I discovered that my car had rolled to a halt right next to a discarded bongo mag. What are the chances of that, eh?

Westy, Australia

I've always disliked pubs and hated the idea of running one. When I was a boy, my father told me that I must stand up to the things I feared, and only in that way would I overcome them. So I opened a pub. It was hell at first, but after five years I am coping quite well, taking one day at a time.

J. Fryer, Leeds

Hit and missus

A poster in my doctors surgery concerning wife beating read 'Don't suffer in Silence'. Well, whenever I punch my missus on the jaw she screams like a fucking banshee. It makes me wonder if doctors know what they're talking about half the time.

R. Crumble, Northants

Keep on trucking

As a truck driver working long hours, I often find myself nodding off at the wheel. However I've found I can relax and keep on driving by simply half closing my eyes and resting my head on a cushion against the window.

J. Manley, Burton on Trent

I think *Viz* and some of its readers are a bit hard on truck drivers. Just recently, a kind trucker who was delivering to my work sold me a backpack jammed full of clothes, footwear and toiletries for £5. Fair enough, most of the contents won't suit me, but it'll make ideal Christmas and birthday presents for my sister. Top bloke.

Stuart Wilson, Scotland

You can choose your friends, but you can't choose your family' they say. Bollocks. I bought my wife from a Thai bride catalogue and made her leave her kids in Bangkok.

G. Barton, e-mail

Puffa puffa mice

Now that scientists have developed an apparent cure for cancer which has been used successfully on mice, isn't it about time the tobacco companies launched mice cigarettes? The potential worldwide must be enormous.

S.T., Chipboard on Tyne

These new 'Gentlemen's Clubs' are a complete con. I went in one the other night and it was full of women. To add insult to injury, most of them were practically naked.

Robert Warren, e-mail

Highland fling

What a rip-off these so called Scottish Widows are. The one they advertise on telly is a real gorgeous, classy tart, but when I fixed myself up with one from the 'Encounters' section of the Glasgow Herald, she turned out to be a right old boiler living in a council flat in Motherwell.

Jamie McSporran, Glasgow

EUROFILE

Your Euro currency questions answered by Ingledew Botterill, Chief Economics Advisor to the Treasury.

Dear Sir,
I intend to holiday on the continent this year. Where do I get Euros from?

Euro notes and coins are widely available from banks, post offices and bureau de changes, although a commission will have to be paid when buying. You can of course avoid this commission by holidaying in Britain.

Dear Sir,
I'm driving through France to Spain this summer. Can I spend French Euros in Spain and vice versa?

Yes, of course, that is the whole point of the system. Any Euro can be spent in any country that has adopted the currency, regardless of where the actual notes or coins originated. You can use French Euros to buy as many straw donkeys and salmonella filled paellas as you like. Spanish Euros will likewise pay for antifreeze-filled French plonk and snails.

Dear Sir,
I recently returned from Rome where I bought a can of coke for 3 Euros. I paid with a 20 Euro note, and was given 50,000 lira change. Was I ripped off?

Confusions such as this will be commonplace whilst there is a period of change over. As a general rule, if you're buying a can of coke in Rome, you're being ripped off. Be careful of toddlers going through your pockets.

Dear Sir,
I'm going to Belfast for a conference in the Spring. Do I need to to buy Euros, as I hear the Irish have adopted the currency?

No, this is a common confusion. The Mick Irish are still using English pounds, it's the Bog Irish that are trotting about with their pockets full of monopoly money.

Dear Sir,
My family have booked a villa in a rural part of mainland Greece. I am a little worried that being in such a rural place, the Euro may not be accepted. Should I take a mixture of currencies, Euros and Drachmas?

To be on the safe side, yes. In theory, every part of Greece should accept Euros, but in rural areas, the truth may be slightly different. Lets face it, when some oily, kebab-chomping copper with a gun is demanding 50 drachmas not to rape your wife and kids, you don't want to find yourself with a wallet full of bumwad from the Bank of Toyland.

Mourning Post

IT'S A shame that Princess Margaret couldn't have witnessed the massive outpouring of indifference that met her timely death recently. As a dreadful person who had no time for anyone else, I'm sure it was what she would have wanted.

J. Geils, Wiltshire

WHEN the sad news of the death of HRH Princess Margaret broke at lunchtime on Saturday 9th February I was devastated, and burst into tears. As a lifelong rugby fan, I was certain that the Challenge Cup Tie between the Bradford Bulls and the Leeds Rhinos would not be shown on Grandstand, but replaced with a respectful tribute to the princess. Fortunately, no one seemed to give two hoots about the old fart and the match was broadcast as scheduled. Well done the BBC.

J. Stark, Bradford

I CANNOT believe that the Royal family gave up so easily and cremated Princess Margaret after her tragic death. Surely they could have put her in a glass coffin and surrounded her by dwarves for a while. At least until the panto season was over.

J.W., Oxford

WHAT is missing from the death of Princess Margaret is a good conspiracy theory. I'll start the ball rolling. Every time the Queen Mum went into hospital to have new hips or blood transfusions, Princess Margaret came out a few days later looking more knackered than ever. I think they were using her as spare parts to keep the Queen Mum going, and now they're going to start on Princess Anne.

Ian Danby, e-mail

THIS nation should hang its head in shame after the death of Princess Margaret. Princess Diana got millions of wailing buffoons signing her book of condolence. Margaret got Jason Donovan and a couple of dozen bemused tourists. And half of them were grinning like Cheshire cats.

H. Robinson, Renfrewshire

PEOPLE have been quick to sneer at the death of HRH Princess Margaret, but she touched a great many lives, and she will be sadly missed. My life will certainly never be the same again. I run an off-licence and tobacconists at the end of her road and I'm finished.

J. Porter, London

I recently had to use a public phone box in London, and was shocked to see a card advertising a 'Spanking by a naughty nurse, any time'. No wonder my mother has been waiting for a hip operation for 18 months when these so-called healthcare professionals are willing to abandon their patients at the drop of a hat in order to attend to someone's sexual lustings.

Matthew Eve, e-mail

Isn't it about time that the late Princess Margaret stopped leeching off society and got herself a proper job? I for one am fed up of paying taxes so she can sit about in an urn on the Queen's mantlepiece all day doing fuck all.

Andrew McKinnon, Dundee

Revelation

The Popemobile has 3-inch thick bullet-proof glass in its windows. There's fucking faith for you.

Doc Choc, Windsor

Utilising the 'law of averages', I've just calculated that at her current shagging rate, Ulrika Jonsson should be slotting me in for a session on or around June 7th 2005. I can't wait.

Adrian Newth, e-mail

Thorough-fair point

All roads lead to Rome, or so they say. Not the A57. I drove along it the other day and ended up in Worksop.

Chas Newman, Sheffield

Everyone is always very quick to point the finger at paedophile priests. But in all fairness, surely half the blame should be on the ten-year-old boys for being just so damned sexy.

Ronald Lilycropp, Canada

I am a good doctor about to be struck off, just for having sex with one of my patients - ten fucking years training down the drain. The British Veterinary Council are cunts.

Paul Murphy, e-mail

I read with incredulity that lorry drivers, in conjunction with the Missing Persons Bureau, will now be travelling the length of the country with hoardings on the sides of their lorries advertising missing persons. Surely this is giving them a licence to boast about their exploits.

Louise Matthews, Leytonstone

With all the problems in the NHS, the staff could increase efficiency at a stroke. When nurses move patients from beds in pairs, instead of lifting on the count of three, they should do it on the count of two, thereby speeding up the process by 33%.

Gabriel Vogt, e-mail

The Opera Babes? 'Opera', yes. But whilst I wouldn't climb over them to get to Luciano Pavarotti, I think the term 'Babes' is stretching it a bit, especially the one on the right.

T. Harris, Wolverhampton

As a mugger, I get really narked when I hear pensioners moaning on about how one of their mates was mugged for 5 pounds. Well, if they would all carry 50 or 100 quid, I wouldn't have to mug so many of them each Friday before going to the pub.

So come on, pensioners! Carry more cash around and reduce the crime rate.

A. Mugger, Walsall

Grave concern

It has been said that alternative comedy, and Ben Elton in particular drove Benny Hill to his grave. That is ridiculous. We did.

B. Blacklock & Sons Funeral Directors, Southampton

Grumble grumble

Why do pornographers insist on using the term 'amateur' when what they really mean is 'ugly'?

J. Deegan, Australia

There don't appear to be any celebrities with cancer at the moment. John Thaw gave up at the drop of a hat, not like your man Roy Castle. At least he made a game of it.

D.J. Furse, e-mail

Tubby comedienne Dawn French is a complete hypocrite. If she really thinks that fat people are so attractive, why didn't she marry Barry White instead of Lenny Henry?

A. Forster, Wolverhampton

The other day I bought a copy of Men Only from my newsagent. Imagine my dismay when I got it home to discover it was full of pictures of women. To make matters worse, most of them weren't wearing a stitch.

Robert Warren, e-mail

Put down boy

People say that every dog has its day. How right they are. We got a dog for Christmas, got bored with it and had it put down on Boxing Day.

Graeme Kenna, Wallasey

I went to see a clairvoyant in 1999. She told me that on September 11th 2001, two passenger jets would crash into the World Trade Centre. I didn't take her seriously at the time, but now I can't forgive myself. If only I had listened I could have sold all my US stocks and shares before that date. But unfortunately I can't turn back time, and I must live with the fact that I lost nearly £280.

Conrad Fitblatt, Kippax

Taking stock

It must be great having your own corner shop. Any time you want anything, you just help yourselves from the shelves. And it's all free! No wonder shopkeepers are always smiling and drive around in Volvo estates.

A. Berry, Grimsby

Heather Mills is a complete hypocrite. Everyone in Britain knows she has only got one leg, so why does she go around with a plastic one, pretending she's got two?

J. Stoppard, Leeds

So what if the Royal Family costs each of us 58p a year? I'd rather it go to them than bloody asylum seekers. These foreigners come over here with all their relations, we give them houses, and they never do a stroke of work, just sponge off the state. They do a marvellous job. God bless 'em.

J. Froud, London

73

The Queen gets 58p per year off every man, woman and child in Britain, does she? Well my three-year-old son gets 10p a week pocket money, which means she takes all his pocket money for 6 weeks. The thieving bitch.

J. Cursitor, Bristol

The reverie's a bastard

Since I won the Football Pools, my life has been like a dream come true. Only the other day I gave my girlfriend a cuddle, but she turned into my dead grandad and started to chase me, and it was like I was running through treacle. And then I realised my maths 'A' level was about to start in ten minutes and I'd done no revision and couldn't find a pen.

R. Baker, Stroud

What's wrong with having Identity Cards? Anyone who objects is obviously a paedophile, and should be chemically castrated.

T. Stomer, Northampton

Mama Cass choked on a sandwich. Jimi Hendrix choked on his own vomit. John Entwhistle, on the other hand, choked on a stripper. What a way to go.

T. Burnside, Leigh

If the makers of Oil of Ulay are so convinced that their spunk-like cream works, why don't they prove it by trying it out on Thora Hird? After a fortnight we'd all know one way or the other.

Mike Thomas, Mid Glamorgan

I've heard that supermarkets waft bakery smells around the store to subconsciously encourage customers to buy bread. I can only conclude that my local Netto supermarket is trying to encourage its customers to buy toilet rolls.

Andy Quin, Huddersfield

Stroke of inspiration

I am left handed, and I have to laugh, because every time I have a wank, it feels like somebody else is doing it.

L. Vincent, Stoke

If you insist on living a 'Shop till you drop' life-style, you will pay the price. I recently saw an elderly gentleman collapse in Tesco, and had no sympathy.

Craig, e-mail

The politically correct lobby would have us believe that the Black and White Minstrel Show was racist. What nonsense. There could have been any number of black faces underneath that make up as membership was open to anyone, regardless of their colour. The same cannot be said for seventies pop band Earth, Wind and Fire. Were there any white faces in their line-up? I think not.

Lt. Col. W Bunter (retd), Aldershot

As expected, the moaning minnies have come out of the woodwork to complain that Sir Mick Jagger has done nothing to deserve his knighthood. Well I disagree. I recently met Marianne Faithfull in the flesh, and never mind a knighthood, I'd want a Dukedom and a life peerage to eat a Mars Bar out of her twat.

John Brown, London

Isn't it marvellous how Falklands hero Simon Weston hasn't aged over the last 20 years? People in Los Angeles would pay a fortune for the secret of eternal youth that Simon is so lucky to possess.

O Lionnel, Essex

Last year I was at an auction in Wisbech while the BBC were filming an episode of Bargain Hunt. However, when it came on the telly last month I was disappointed to see that they didn't show the box of porn that sparked a bidding frenzy and went for a handsome £250. Even Dickinson put in a couple of cheeky bids for the 'box of delights'.

Mr Allgood, e-mail

SPORT TALK

The World Cup may have gone, but England is still smarting from the Ronaldhino free kick that put us out of the tournament. Was it a goalkeeping blunder by David Seaman, or a spectacular fluke shot by the zombie-faced Brazilian? We've been inundated with letters giving your point of view.

...I used to love watching David Seaman on Match of the Day. The next time I see his face on telly, I'll put a bloody brick through the screen... and send him the bill!

R. Winston, London

...I was surprised that Seaman had the nerve to show his face in this country again. If I were him, I would have done the decent thing and put myself into permanent exile.

T. Pierce, Widdecombe

...Watching Seaman let that goal in made me sick to my stomach. I think he should be put on the sexual offenders register.

Jan Stewer, Wimbledon

...If Seaman had spent a little less time having his hair cut like a girl, and a little more time moving backwards towards the far post, maybe it would have been England's name on the World Cup instead of Brazil's.

Dan Whidden, Derby

...Seaman earns a fortune playing for Arsenal. If he had a shred of decency in his body, he would spend every last penny on research into time travel, then go back in time to just before the kick was taken and stand a little nearer to the back post.

William Brewer, Devon

...Seaman has apologised for the second Brazilian goal. But it takes two to tango. What about the man who actually kicked the ball into the net? He showed no regret whatsoever. In fact, he looked rather pleased with himself.

H. Hawk Leicester

...I think Seaman should be hanged on Match of the Day. And Gary Lineker could pull the lever. This would not only prevent him messing up again, but would act as a deterrent to other goalkeepers thinking about letting in a similar goal.

Peter Gurney, Hull

...Gordon Banks would have saved that shot, and he's only got one eye. That makes Banks twice the keeper that the two-eyed Seaman will ever be.

Thomas Cobbley, Dublin

...I don't blame Seaman for the appalling blunder that let in Brazil's second goal. I blame his hairdresser. If, instead of letting his ponytail dangle down his back, he had gelled it into a spike above his head, he could have used it to tip the ball over the crossbar.

Ann Dall, Wales

...Let's all stop attacking David Seaman. It's only a game after all. The most important things were that all the matches were played in good spirit and everyone taking part enjoyed themselves. And that the fucking krauts lost in the final.

Peter Davy, Edinburgh

Dulux say 'you find the colour, we'll match it.' Well I found the colour, on one of their fucking colour charts, and they couldn't even match that, so what chance they've got with the handle off an inflatable boat I don't know.

Dan Sullivan, West Bromwich
PS. My lounge does not look 'Aztec Gold'. It's fucking orange.

I am a zoo keeper and spend my day feeding the penguins. When I go home at night, I feed the seal. That's because I'm married to the pop singer Seal, out of Adamski and he always wants his tea! Can any of your readers beat that?

Vera Seal (out of Adamski), London

Summit to think about

If heat rises, how come the top of Mount Everest is so fucking cold?

Sir E. Hilary, New Zealand

We read a lot in the newspapers about strategies to prevent another September 11th happening, but upon checking my calendar to-

day, I noticed that yet another one is planned for later this year. Will they never learn!

Moose, e-mail

On a recent Jonathan Ross show, David Bowie said he doesn't change his baby daughter's nappy. What a hypocrite. He wasn't afraid of shit when he was a bummer, why now?

N Foukes, Cardiff

I would like to inform tennis racquet manufacturers Slazenger that I just just spent £21.95 on a Wilson racquet because their own product at £19.95 had a picture of Tim Henman on it. If Slazenger want to continue losing business, then I suggest they continue getting Mr Huffy to endorse their products. On the same note, if Wilson decided to double the cost of their racquets, I'm sure most people would happily pay.

B. Henry, Hexham

They say that carbon monoxide is the silent killer in the home. Not in my house it's not. It was my husband Fred.

Rose West, Durham

78

I have to complain at the way the English language is being hijacked by all and sundry. In my youth, gay meant happy. Now it's solely used to describe the activity of a buggerist. Let's say it how it is.

Colonel AKP Hepcott-White (Rtd), Surrey

There's nothing worse than constipation on your big day" the advert for Senecot says. Surely the shits would be far worse.

Dave Oliver, Hartlepool

There is something wrong with my new girlfriend. Each time I try and stick my cock in her mouth, she turns her head to put it in her ear. Do you think it's a fetish?

R Skelton, Plymouth

I'm not happy with the way our beautiful language is being taken from us. In my youth, foxy meant fox-like. Now it has connotations of sexual attraction. I can't describe a small reddish-brown dog as being foxy anymore without being taken for some sort of bestialist.

Colonel AKP Hepcott-White (Rtd), Surrey

I think the bin men in my area have got a cheek going on strike for being underpayed. They only work one day a week, the lazy fuckers.

Patrick Millner, e-mail

How come grumble vid star Ben Dover can manage to mess around with loads of birds just by dishing a few crappy compliments about? I told Doreen (my mate Dave's nan) that her homemade fairycakes were delicious. I thought I was well in, but she went berserk when I woke her up at 3am by slapping my cock on her chin.

W. Hardman, e-mail

When I was a boy, galvanise meant to coat iron with a thin layer of zinc to prevent rust. Now, apparently, it means to rouse a group of people forcibly by shock or excitement. How much longer are we going to allow our language to be stolen from us?

Colonel AKP Hepcott-White (Rtd), Surrey

They say that those who live by the sword will die by the sword. What nonsense. I'm a blacksmith specializing in period weaponry, and I've just been diagnosed with terminal cancer of the throat.

M. Plywood, Yorkshire

He'll get by with a little help from the lottery

I think it's a disgrace that Lottery money is to be spent renovating Paul McCartney's council house in Liverpool. With all his money he could easily afford to do it himself.

J. Ninety,
Weston Supermarionation

When my grandad died, everyone said that that his little dog Paddy, a faithful companion for 14 years, would die of a broken heart. But they were all wrong, as we had him put down the day after the funeral.

T. Walker, London

Whoever says what goes up, must come down has clearly never stuck a milk bottle up their arse.

P. Purvis, London

My girlfriend has just dumped me. She wrote saying she "had to really leave because a no-good-fucking-smartarse-scumbag-wanker wasn't someone to spend a life with". Do you think I should mention that she has split an infinitive AND ended a sentence with a preposition when I write begging her to stay with me? Or should I correct her later?

Darren Anderson,
Thornton-Cleveleys

Corny

I think anyone who pays good money to see a chiropodist needs to have their feet examined. Or something like that.

John O'Connor, e-mail

On the 11th September last year, I moved into a flat with my girlfriend and, knowing full well I would be expected to remember the anniversary of us moving together, I was racking my brains to think of a way to remember the date. Imagine my relief when I finally got the TV wired up in our new living room and saw the tragic events unfolding in New York, on a day that none of us will ever forget for many years to come.

Dave Willis, e-mail

Another fine mess

I wonder if any of your readers could help me. I am seeking sponsors to help me pay the latest fine handed to me by Weston Magistrates Court (£75 for committing a 'Public Order' offence while drunk). If anyone could help, in return for your sponsorship I will gladly mention you or your company name the next time I am up before the magestrates.

Andy Quinn
Weston-super-Mare

I'm all for change and progress, but was in two minds about whether we should adopt the Euro until I heard that each country was allowed to produce their own. Now I'm all for it, as it will allow us to join a united Europe whilst retaining our own Queen's head on the currency. It also means that we can easily identify the notes and coins produced in other EU countries and re-fuse to accept them in our shops.

J. Butler, Derby

Martin Brundle sang the praises of the 16 strong Ferrari pit crew during the Italian Grand Prix last week after they changed Michael Schumacher's tyres in 8.4 seconds. That's nothing. I stopped at some lights for 5 seconds in the centre of Liverpool last week, and some kids had my hub caps, wing mirrors, radio and my briefcase out the boot. And there was only 3 of the bastards.

Bill Moss, e-mail

Hats off to Sir Alex Ferguson who treated the false accusations of sexual harassment against him with the contempt they deserved. He showed that if you are innocent of a crime, then you have absolutely nothing whatsoever to worry about.

Barry George,
Belmarsh Prison

I think it's marvellous that we see so many women bus drivers these days. It's about time that women were given the opportunity to show

81

that they can perform perfectly well in what were previously thought of as male only jobs. Good on 'em and more power to their elbow, I say. Mind you, I'm glad they only let them out in the little 25 seat city-hoppers. I wouldn't fancy being near one behind the wheel of a double decker when she's trying to back it into the depot.

J. Lightfoot, Newcastle

I was surprised to learn the other day that co-median Richard Blackwood is the half-brother of supermodel Naomi Campbell. It must be quite un-usual to have two such multitalent-less people in the same family.

A. Sommers, Carlisle

Every time I visit the hairdressers, the gorgeous blonde girl who cuts my hair thoughtfully gives me a tissue when she has finished. Obvi-ously, she knows I'm going straight home to have a wank over her. The last time I went, however, she wasn't there and a bloke with a moustache cut my hair instead. Imagine my dis-gust when he also gave me a tissue. I don't think I'll be going back there again.

Mick Sterbs, Coventry

Phoney lines

The girls on the 'Live 1-2-1, 30 second instant cum lines' are not really 19-year-old blonde Swedish nymphos with a 38-22-36 figure. They're more likely to be fat 49-year-old boilers with saggy tits, big arses and treble chins. I should know, because my missus is one.

A. Berry, Grimsby

Opportunity knockout

They say that in a fight, you should use your opponent's weight against them. That's all very well, but it didn't do my uncle any good when he was attacked in a pub by Lena Zavaroni.

P. Miller, London

Radio 4 Sexual Problems
with
Dr David Jackson

Dear Dr Jackson,
I suffer from premature ejaculation during the shipping forecast. I set my radio alarm for 5.30 am each day to allow my wife to perform fellatio on me during the forecast. She begins her foreplay when the music starts, I become aroused between 'Viking' and 'Forties' and regularly come in her mouth around 'Fastnet' or 'Mallin'.

Friends of mine tell me they can hold on until 'Faroes' or even 'South East Iceland'. Is this macho boasting or am I abnormal?

B. Vine-Miller, Devon

Do YOU have a sexual problem relating to Radio 4 that you'd like to share with Dr Jackson? Do you have difficulty maintaining an erection during 'Midweek' with Libby Purves. Perhaps you fear your wife is having an affair with the presenters of 'Veg Talk'. Or maybe you can only become aroused during 'Moneybox Live' if you wear your wife's clothes.

Write to him at: **Radio 4 Sexual Problems, Viz Comic, PO Box 1PT, Newcastle upon Tyne, NE99 1PT.**

Dr Jackson regrets that he cannot answer any problems either personally, or in the pages of the magazine.

Smile, gentlemen please!

★ In my efforts to assist in your quest for smiles lacking in sincerity, it would appear that in this picture of Cllr Nigel Barron (below) from the Thurrock Gazette, I chanced upon a rare treat. But to find it in the very next column to one of Cllr Peter Maynard was nothing short of divine intervention.

Andy Slocombe, Grays

★ On the subject of insincere smiles, I spotted this photo of Tony Blair, taken shortly after the petrol crisis. He may be kidding himself that it's a convincing grin, but you can't fuel us, Tony.

**Dave Saunders
Cricklewood**

This Harry Potter film is all well and good, but I can't help thinking it's all a bit far fetched. I mean, how many schools do you know where there's a ginger kid with two mates?

Tim Woods, e-mail

The press has been complaining that Michael Jackson was cruel to put a towel over his baby's head before dangling it off a fourth floor balcony. I think he deserves a round of applause. If the tot had been able to see how far he could fall, he would have been terrified. Jacko showed responsibility and fatherly kindness by covering his head before pulling his cheeky stunt.

Ron Hubbard, Cardiff

Has anyone lost a flat, orange cat and some flies in the car park of Llantrisant Tescos? I found them yesterday and wonder if there is a reward.

Kris, Pontyclun

If spare ribs are spare, how come my local chinese restaurant charges a fortune for them?

Ching Woo, Chingford

I am only just getting over the sad demise of the TV producer Desmond Wilcox. I always hoped that he would outlive his wife Esther Rantzen by many years.

Hedgepig, e-mail

Regarding the issue of whether Gibraltar should join Spain or remain part of Britain, if I lived there I would opt to join with Spain. Just think how much better the weather would be.

Philip Welton, Stoke on Trent

Just dessert

As I walked into the kitchen this morning I was horrified to find my elderly mother haemorrhaging from the mouth, coughing up pus into a bowl and screaming uncontrollably. Imagine my relief when I spotted a cherry amongst the sticky mess, and realised she was only eating a trifle, and shrieking with delight.

J.F. Taylor, Bury

You'd think that after 23 years, some of these so called 'Children in Need' might have grown up like the rest of us.

Moose, Valley Park

Only the other day I came home from work and found a mixture of men's and women's clothing scattered about my lounge. Imagine my surprise when I discovered my boyfriend upstairs, naked in our bed having sex with my best friend. I hit the roof. However, he soon cleared it all up by explaining that 'It was only a bit of fun, and it meant nothing'. How foolish I felt for making such a fuss.

Alicia Trump,
North Berkshire

My middle name is Kenelm, which is Anglo Saxon for 'Bold Helmet'. Can any of your readers beat that?

Matthew Hunter, e-mail

I would just like to say what a load of bollocks these hygiene laws are. I have been a baker for nearly 12 years now, and not once have I washed my hands after having a shit. So far, no one has complained.

F. U. Bowen, Essex

I was sitting watching the football on the BBC last night, and it said you could get 'interactive' by pressing the red button on the remote. I pressed mine and the telly went off.

Ken Topping, e-mail

The government recently announced that first-time burglars will no longer receive a custodial sentence, but will be given community service instead. With that in mind, I am looking for three other law-abiding citizens to have a crack at nicking the Crown Jewels from the Tower of London. The rewards are untold wealth, and the worst that can happen is that you would have to spend thirty days picking up crisp packets. Any takers?

Gary Beard, e-mail

I was recently convicted for a string of armed robberies and was sentenced to be detained at Her Majesty's pleasure. I know I've done wrong, but the thought of the Queen sitting in a palace, smirking at my plight really galls me.

T. Francis, HMP Durham

I was heartened by the actions of a Millwall FC supporter who came into my local pub last Saturday, took two balls from the pool table, slipped them into a sock and left looking for "Northern cunt Preston fans". Imagine our surprise when he returned a few minutes later, set the balls back on the table and apologised for the disruption to our game. His conduct was a credit to Millwall FC. What a pity certain other of their supporters don't behave in such a courteous manner.

P Pugnano, Preston

I just went for a shit and it smelt exactly the same as the Chicken Jalfrezi I had last night - absolutely gorgeous.

Ed Bowden, Bromley

What a racquet

Why do women tennis players make such a loud grunt every time they hit the ball? If the act of hitting a ball is so difficult for them, perhaps they should stick to more ladylike pastimes such as knitting or dressmaking.

Ric Porter, London

How come every time I buy a bongo mag, the newsagent looks at me like I'm a dirty bastard? He's the one profiteering from such filth.

Joel Young, Middlesbrough

Fallen angel

Teenage singing sensation Charlotte Church's behaviour in Cincinatti the other week was deplorable. In refusing to meet disabled fans after a concert, she showed herself up as a spoilt brat. What this young lady needs is some good old fashioned discipline. I would happily put Miss Church across my knee, lift up her skirt and spank her bare behind until she learned some manners.

Torbjorn Abercromby, Manchester

Congratulations to Crimewatch for staging a reconstruction of the horrifying tiara theft at the Scottish home of the late Princess of Wales's mother Mrs Shand-Kydd. It's heartening to know that interest is being taken in property crime perpetrated against elderly ladies. Doubtless the BBC will soon be popping round to my Granny's flat in the west end of Newcastle to reconstruct some of the dozen or so break-ins the poor cow's had in the last 18 months.

J. Thomas, Newcastle

Nitty gritty

I wonder if any of your readers could advise me on a matter of etiquette. My girlfriend was giving me a blowjob the other day, when I noticed a small creature, obviously a nit, crawling through her hair. I'm not sure whether or not I should tell her. I don't want to risk hurting her feelings as she is my wife's best friend.

Christopher Hampshire, Bristol

S urely it would make sense to simply nuke the Middle East. Then all the sand would turn to dunes of glass that you could ski on, providing you lined your skis with velvet. And you could find oil just by wandering around looking down.

Neil Weatherall, e-mail

W hat a lot of n o n s e n s e this tantric sex is. So Sting can delay his climax for seven hours. That's nothing. I've been banging my missus for forty years and she's not had an orgasm yet.

P Collins, Colchester

P sychologists say that men who like women with large breasts are suffering from an Oedipal complex. What bollocks. I like big tits, and I don't want to shag my mam. Her tits are tiny.

Joel Young, e-mail

N ow that increasing numbers of celebrities are being accused by the newspapers of paedophilia, I find it quite refreshing that John Leslie is only accused of raping mature women well over the age of consent. Hats off to him.

Mark, e-mail

Dad to be gay

These people who object to gay men bringing up children, saying they will lack female role models show a staggering level of ignorance. Surely they'll get all the feminine influence they need with both parents skipping around the house in high heeled shoes and dresses.

T. Kavanagh, Wapping

I was delighted when the kind people at the Inland Revenue wrote to me recently, telling me that my tax return was 'outstanding', particularly since I can't even remember sending it in.

Tom McCann, Wokingham

Clint Made My Day

My grandson recently installed a security camera on my front door. "Just press 9 on the remote when someone knocks," he said. "Then you can check who's there on the TV." Last Tuesday, there was a knock on the door. Would you believe Clint Eastwood had called on me to pay a visit! However, by the time I got to the door he was gone. And only this morning, Fern Britton came round, and I don't even know her. I must have kept her waiting quite a while, as she was sitting on a sofa she had brought along with her. Have any other readers had surprise visits from celebrities?

Florence Lilian Davenport,
e-mail

According to the HSBC, the rudest thing you can do in Thailand is show the soles of your feet. What nonsense. On my last trip to Bangkok, I shat on a ladyboy's tits whilst his sister wanked me into their mum's hair.

B. Shipton, Leigh on Sea

If my wife is reading this, could I just point out that that, yes, sticking my thumb up her arse whilst shagging her IS completely necessary.

Kid, e-mail

The government say that benefit fraud is costing every household in Britain about £80 per month. Nonsense. I'm up 300 quid a week.

A Collins, Liverpool

I'm a pensioner and the other day I opened the door to find four 12-year-olds in tracksuits asking to read my meter. Hats off to the gas board for giving these youngsters such valuable work experience.

Mrs Earnshaw, Frome

Like everyone, I felt very sorry for Christopher Reeve suffering paralysis after his tragic riding accident. Since conventional medical treatment has had little or no effect, perhaps now is the time to try something more radical. As a doctor, I have heard of many cases of people suffering amnesia after a blow on the head, only for their memory to return after a further blow. Perhaps if the ex-Superman star were to fall off another horse he might regain full use of his body. It's worth a go.

Dr Andy Quinn, Huddersfield

Tuppence on rates

I've just recieved my new local council tax bill, and I note that it has gone up by £200 this year. This is in part to fund a new lesbian drop-in centre. I'm not opposed to this in principle, but I think after forking out for it, the least they could do is let me in to watch

B. Aldiss, Lambeth

It's been one sad tragedy after another for your average Beatles fan. What with the slaying of John Lennon by a crazed maniac, and the more recent loss of George Harrison through cancer. I only hope that the next Beatle death can be a little more cheery. Perhaps Paul McCartney can ski off a cliff and leave a comical spread-eagle shape in the snow below. Or possibly Ringo Starr could be electrocuted by a Las

Vegas slot-machine, causing his eyes to spin in their sockets before finally settling on two 'jackpot' signs, setting off a cascade of silver dollars spilling out of his mouth.

Andy Epwurf, Castleford

These days, most shops have wheelchair access, but once inside the shop, the needs of the disabled are all but forgotten. Whilst in my newsagents the other day, I realised how difficult it must be for someone in a wheelchair to purchase a top shelf magazine. They would have to ask someone to pass it down which would cause great embarrassment.

Wouldn't it be a good idea if newsagents had a pneumatic ramp by the magazines to lift wheelchairs up to the top shelf. It could be fitted with flashing lights and a klaxon to warn other customers to keep clear of the mechanism when in operation.

Steve Dawson, e-mail

Can you settle an argument? My wife says I'm a drunken bastard for coming home at 3 in the morning and pissing in the wardrobe. I say she's a lazy cow who never makes any effort to look nice, and if she gave me a bit now and then I wouldn't have to go looking for it elsewhere. Who is correct?

T. Arnold, London

I don't know why Heather Mills is so concerned about land mines. She's only half as much at risk from them as everybody else.

**_J. Jordan,
Leeds_**

I watched the much-hyped 'Walking With Cavemen' last week with some disappointment. Where were all the dinosaurs? If the producers had done their research to the same standard as those who made The Flintstones, these mistakes wouldn't have occurred. Or perhaps it was penny pinching by the BBC that has once again affected programme quality.

David Hershman, e-mail

On hearing Pink's song 'Don't Let Me Get Me' where she begs for 'a day in the life of someone else' I was filled with pity. I wrote to her offering to spend a day mucking about in a music studio, while she could spend eight hours packing cheese before returning home to an alcoholic mother and her local felon boyfriend. I have yet to receive a response.

A Dawes, Northumberland

In the unlikely event that S a m a n t h a Mumba ever turns up at my house whilst my wife is out and demands a portion, this is the order I will do her in: arse, gob, arse. If I have any left I will do her arse again.

Paul Evans, e-mail

I felt that the public reaction to the death of Princess Diana was a little over the top. My wife, who was a thoroughly decent woman, died last week, and who made any fuss about her? Certainly not me.

Andrew Dunn, Kent

What a con this so-called evaporated milk is. I opened a tin of it the other day and it was still completely full.

Jules, Great Yarmouth

Nan the wiser

My Nan always used to tell us that you get what you pay for. Well not these days you don't. I bought a porn video called 'Under 19s Anal Heaven' from a shop in Nottingham, and the tape turned out to be a chuffing blank. It's a good job my Nan's dead or she'd be eating her words.

Pol Brun, London

The double standards employed by the Greek authorities never cease to amaze me. Whilst on holiday in Corfu this year, I witnessed young women sunbathing topless in full view of everyone, including young children. Many of them wore bikini bottoms that barely covered their buttocks, and the authorities did nothing. However, on the same beach my husband, who had the decency to remain fully clothed, was arrested by police for masturbating in the privacy of his own trousers.

Mrs. E. Nogg, Leeds

Grinning twat

So Richard Whiteley reckons he has appeared on British telly more times than anyone else over the last thirty-five years. You'd think by now he would actually be able to do it, wouldn't you?

A. Mitchell, Grimsby

Last year, my wife and I told the neighbours we were going to the South of France for two weeks and made a big show of loading up the car and setting off. Later, having pushed the car into a nearby canal, we returned under the cover of darkness. After burying the suitcases in the garden we re-entered the house through a downstairs window and hid behind the settee. For days we kept perfectly still and quiet, defecating into plastic bags to avoid flushing the lavatory. However, we were discovered after ten days when the neighbour, who had come in to water our plants, saw my wife's foot poking out from behind the settee. Next year we shall be more careful and hide in the wardrobe.

G. Poad, Farnborough

I recently attended a bull fight during a holiday in Spain. I went with an open mind, but I can honestly say that I have never been so appalled and upset by an event in all my life. It cost £8 to get in, a can of coke was another £1.50, and I was sat so far at the back that I couldn't see the cows getting stabbed.

Victoria Gardener, Sussex

Please find enclosed one of the cheekiest unsolicited adverts for a crap product ever to fall out of a newspaper. "Marketing break-through"– too right, because if they shift just one of these to anyone who has even one of their marbles left, then they're the king of sales-men.

Stuart Edwards, Hertfordshire

Amazing "Dish" Antenna Works Indoors!

Only £5 +&&

Works like any ordinary rabbit ears.
Put one on every TV in your home.
Compatible with all TV's
Works entirely via "RF" technology —to capture signals right out of the air!
You pay NO satellite fees because you DON'T use satellite signals!
Not technical razzle-dazzle but a marketing breakthrough.

#J54220 TV "Dish" Antenna £5

With reference to the above letter. I think it's very sad how cynical people are in this day and age. I think the Amazing Indoor TV Dish Antenna, costing £5 and promising to get you terrestrial channels plus all satellite channels free of charge really will work.

J. Booth, Wednesbury

We all saw the Queen Mum enjoying her 100th birthday, but let's not forget the many other centegenarians who have celebrated their happy day. Here's one having a whale of a time recently in Cleveland.

Sarah Morgan,
Stockton-on-Tees

These speed cameras are a complete con. Not only do they take about five weeks, but they cost £75 a throw.

B. Badger, Ford

94

Last week Britain snapped up the world record for serial killing when Dame Janet Smith's enquiry into the Harold Shipman murders concluded that the mad medic's stiff count was a whopping **260!** We went on the streets to find out your views.

...SHIPMAN may have killed over 260 people, but they were all knocking on a bit, so if you add up the total number of years of life he deprived people of, it's not that much. A life sentence for a middle-aged man seems a little harsh under the circumstances.

J. Barnstaple, Devon

...COMMENTATORS are saying that alarm bells should have rung when the death toll in Shipman's surgery was higher than the national average. Perhaps they should have an electrician in to check the circuits and the wiring to make sure a tragedy of such enormity doesn't happen again.

P. Balsa, London

...WITH the National Health Service in the state it is, the failure for alarm bells to ring at the start of Shipman's killing spree doesn't surprise me at all. I have fitted my elderly mother with her own alarm system. If her doctor tries to kill her, a loud siren goes off in her knickers and a blue strobe light begins to flash on her hat.

T. Widnes, Hartlepool

...PEOPLE are very quick to criticise the bad things Shipman has done, but they must be balanced against all the good that he did. I went to see him in 1996 with an ear infection. He prescribed a course of Otomize ear spray and Amoxycillin tablets and it was gone within 3 days. He may have killed my granny and her next door neighbour the following year, but I won't hear a word against him.

T. Plywood, Manchester

...IT IS beyond me to imagine what sort of twisted pleasure Shipman could have derived from watching his victims die. I think he should be publicly hung. Very slowly. With piano music.

T. Gilbert, London

...THE INQUIRY has blamed Shipman for hundreds of murders without the need for a trial. It seems a shame to let the opportunity to finger him for a few other crimes go to waste. For instance, four years ago, the radio was stolen from my car in Moss Side, a deed which could easily have been the work of Shipman's evil hand.

P. Dentrisangle, Wales

95